WWJ, The Detroit News: The History Of Radiophone Broadcasting By The Earliest And Foremost Of Newspaper Stations; Together With Information On Radio For Amateur And Expert

The Detroit News

"WWJ—The Detroit News"

The History of Radiophone
Broadcasting by the Earliest
and Foremost of Newspaper
Stations; Together With
Information on Radio for
Amateur and Expert.

by

The Radio Staff

of

The Detroit News

Published by
The Evening News Association
Detroit, Mich.
1922

Officers of The Detroit News

Printing Statement:

Due to the very old age and scarcity of this book,
many of the pages may be hard to read due to the
blurring of the original text, possible missing pages,
missing text, dark backgrounds and other issues
beyond our control.

Because this is such an important and rare work, we
believe it is best to reproduce this book regardless of
its original condition.

Thank you for your understanding.

James Edmund Scripps, 1835-1906.

The founder of The Detroit News was among the earliest to recognize the possibilities of radio communication; and contributed funds for pioneer experimentation. His son, William E. Scripps, vice-president and managing director of The News, is chiefly responsible for the establishment and development of Station WWJ.

CONTENTS

ILLUSTRATIONS

The World's Greatest Newspaper Plant

The paper warehouse and main building of The Detroit News occupy a city block, 300 by 280 feet square.

The Growth of a Service

THE DETROIT NEWS was the first newspaper in the world to install a radio broadcasting station, and the first to increase its social usefulness by furnishing such a service to the public. When broadcasting was inaugurated in the summer of 1920, wireless telephony, although it had reached a commercial stage and was already the hobby of a few enthusiastic experimenters, still remained a mystery to the community in general and was looked upon by many as possibly a familiar source of enjoyment to their grandchildren but of no particular present importance. This sentiment was virtually changed overnight when, in August, 1920, The Detroit News installed its first transmitting station and commenced its regular broadcasting.

The original apparatus consisted of a De Forest Type OT-10 transmitter, using a 200-wave length. Its range was limited, being, under the best of conditions, not more than 100 miles; and at the time there were, approximately, only 300 operators receiving in the territory covered. The transmission set was in place ready for operation on Aug. 20, 1920, but no announcement was made to the public until a series of experimental concerts had been conducted over a period of 10 days. These concerts were enjoyed by no one save such amateurs as happened to be listening in. Everything was found to be satisfactory, and on Aug. 31, which was primary election day, it was announced that the returns, local, state and congressional, would be sent to the public that night by means of the radio.

The News on Wednesday, Sept. 1, 1920, carried the following announcement:

"The sending of the election returns by The Detroit News' radiophone Tuesday night was fraught with romance and must go down in the history of man's con-

quest of the elements as a gigantic step in his progress.
In the four hours that the apparatus, set up in an out-of-
the-way corner of The News Building, was hissing and
whirring its message into space, few realized that a
dream and a prediction had come true. The news of the
world was being given forth through this invisible trumpet to the waiting crowds in the unseen market place.":

It was Aug. 31, then, which marked the beginning of
radiophone broadcasting by the press as a public service.
The dream of actual vocal contact between points far
distant and without any tangible physical union had come
true on an astonishingly large scale. The public of Detroit
and its environs was on that date made to realize that
what had been a laboratory curiosity was to become a
commonplace of everyday life, and that the future held
extraordinary developments which would affect all
society.

Every week day since that date, and latterly on Sundays, too, The News has broadcast a program to an ever-
increasing audience. There has been no interruption in
this service and the programs have constantly become
more extensive and elaborate.

At first the concerts were confined entirely to phonograph music. Two programs were broadcast daily—one
at 11:30 a. m. and the other at 7 p. m.—and after a time,
speakers and singers were occasionally obtained to enter-
tain the invisible audience.

Soon reports commenced coming in from outlying
communities that the concerts were being successfully
received and enthusiastically enjoyed. The radio has
become such a familiar affair in so short a space of time
that it seems odd to consider how remarkable this was
regarded at the time. The thing from the first held the
element of magic. The local receiving set became the
center of wondering interest in the little suburban towns.
The interest grew and dealers reported a demand for
radio materials.

Then the Steamer W. A. Bradley reported through
the Marconi station at Ecorse, near Detroit on the west,

that the music of a News concert had been received on the vessel as she steamed along through the night in the middle of Lake St. Clair. This, somehow, impressed the public as even more remarkable than sending the music over land although, of course, it was not. But the notion of a ship far off from land actually comprehending the words spoken and the music played in a little room of a building in a great city seemed a peculiarly significant demonstration of the victory over distance and darkness.

During the first week of broadcasting a party at the home of C. F. Hammond, 700 Parker Avenue, Detroit, danced to music sent out by the News apparatus and this was considered the local beginning of the social aspect of wireless telephony.

The man in the street, traditionally skeptical, was much impressed when, in October, 1920, the results of the World Series base ball contest between Cleveland and Brooklyn were instantly sent out to the waiting base ball enthusiasts. The first returns of a national election ever broadcast were given by The News in November of the same year, when hundreds of partisan voters held receivers to their ears and were informed by the voice through the ether that Harding had rolled up an enormous majority over Cox.

When Christmas season came around in 1920 the number of radio amateurs had greatly increased in Detroit and the surrounding communities. Small boys were becoming enthusiasts and Santa Claus remembered a great many with receiving sets, thus adding members to The News' radio family. Special holiday music, appropriate to the season, was broadcast.

On New Year's Day of 1921 The News said:

"For the first time, as far as known, a human voice singing a New Year's melody of cheer went out across uncounted miles over the invisible ether that is the medium of the wireless telephone when Louis Colombo, Detroit attorney and famous baritone, sent his resonant tones into the mouthpiece at the office of The Detroit News at midnight, Friday."

And an astonishing achievement was considered to have been performed when those in attendance at a banquet at the Masonic Temple heard a concert received at the banquet hall by means of a three-wire aerial strung along the ceiling.

By this time the original transmitting set in the News station was found to be inadequate for the increasing requirements and it was almost entirely rebuilt. In the following June a two-wire antenna, 290 feet in length, was stretched between The News Building and the Hotel Fort Shelby. Soon reports began to come in from distant points that The News' concerts were being heard plainly. Belleville, Ill., sent word that the concerts were enjoyed there, and Atlanta, Ga., delighted the News operators by announcing that the broadcasting was carrying successfully to that "distant place." Meantime, The News' receiving set was catching wireless telegraph messages from remote radio stations, including the U. S. Navy station at Bordeaux, France, and stations in Nauen, Germany, Rome and Hawaii.

The Detroit News decided to organize its programs on a more elaborate scale. These had previously been restricted, principally to phonograph music and news bulletins, but now musicians were added and theatrical talent booked from Detroit playhouses. The first noted literary man to send out his compositions through the ether to thousands of ear-pieces was Edmund Vance Cooke, the poet.

So it went until the end of 1921. In December the present ambitious program was instituted. By this time the radio department demanded the entire time of a radiophone editor and two technical men, which staff has at present grown to not fewer than eleven persons regularly employed, the department being divided into four sections—administrative, editorial, program and technical. There is a supervising editor, two reporters, a secretary, stenographers as required, a program director and assistant, and a chief radio engineer and four engineer-operators.

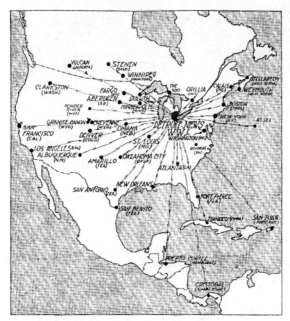

The Conquest of Space.

A few of the remote points which have heard WWJ Broadcasts.

The department occupies 3,003 square feet of floor space on the fourth floor of The News Building, divided into editorial and executive offices, instrument and operating room, laboratory, auditorium and producing studios.

Today phonograph music occupies an incidental place on the daily schedule and the programs are filled by city, state and national celebrities, prominent clergymen, vocal and instrumental artists, and public figures. When the

little microphone stood in the presence of Madame Emma
Calve recently, she sang to the greatest audience of her
life—over WWJ. When Lillian and Dorothy Gish and
David W. Griffith came to the News phonitorium to
talk intimately with the radio family, Lillian remarked.
"Oh, this is as nice as the nicest movie studio." When
Sir Philip Gibbs, the famous war correspondent, talked
to the continent at this station, he marveled. "In Eng-
land," he said, "the radiophone has not even begun to
develop as such a magnificent social service."

Another point in the program expansion of December,
1921, was the procuring of Finzel's Orchestra and other
musical organizations with numerous members. These
orchestras furnish varied numbers, including dance
music, by radio, and it became common for Detroiters to
hold parties in their homes and step to their favorite
orchestras. The second Christmas concert presented by
The News, Dec. 24, 1922, included songs by carolers and
addresses by Alex. J. Groesbeck, Governor of Michigan;
James Couzens, Mayor of Detroit, and the Rt. Rev. Fr.
John P. McNichols, president of the University of
Detroit. A feature of the Christmas Eve service was the
broadcasting of the music played by the chimes in the
steeple of the Fort Street Presbyterian Church, located
across the street from The News Building.

In February, 1922, The News first broadcast a concert
by the Detroit Symphony Orchestra. Thereafter every
program presented by that splendid organization was
sent to music lovers, not only in Detroit but over half of
the North American continent. Expressions of enthusiastic appreciation from persons in all walks of life have fol-
lowed this development of The News' radio service.
Contributions for the support of the orchestra have come
from grateful people in a score of states, and even in
Cuba, who have thus been enabled to hear finer music
and better played than could ever be heard in the small
towns where they make their residences. The radiophone has opened new worlds of appreciation to music-
hungry folk.

Since the beginning of 1922, The News has been able to provide its audience with an impressive array of diversified numbers, undreamed of in the early days of broadcasting. The eminent Shakespearean artists, Edward H. Sothern and his wife, Julia Marlowe, gave their classical interpretations over this radiophone during one of their engagements in Detroit. Walter Hampden, the new Shakespearean star, did likewise. Among the other noted actors who made their radio debut in the News transmitting studio are Frank Tinney, Van and Schenk, Lew Fields, Will Rogers and Percy Wenrich.

During Lent, 1922, the leading clergymen of all denominations provided sermons as a feature of every evening program. The Rt. Rev. Michael J. Gallagher, Roman Catholic Bishop of the Diocese of Detroit; the Rt. Rev. Charles D. Williams, Episcopal Bishop, and Bishop Theodore S. Henderson, of the Methodist Church, are among the divines who have made addresses.

In that Easter season, The News entered into arrangements with St. Paul's Episcopal Cathedral, whereby the radio public enjoyed the Easter Cantata sung in that church on Palm Sunday, and heard the Cathedral's morning and evening services on Easter Day. Thus the Cathedral was no longer one merely of stone of architectural dimensions, but one whose mystic walls encompassed most of the continent. Cathedral services were thereafter regularly broadcast.

University extension, early in 1922, became a part of the function of this station. Speakers have been listed from the University of Michigan at Ann Arbor and the Michigan Agricultural College at Lansing, including administrative and executive heads and numerous members of the faculties.

The cap-sheaf was added, however, when, on May 28, 1922, The Detroit News Orchestra appeared for the first time in the studio. This, the first radio orchestra ever organized, is a 16-piece symphonic ensemble, composed of soloists of note. Its members were drawn almost exclusively from the Detroit Symphony Orchestra, but

Some Illustrious Personages Heard Over WWJ.

Some Illustrious Personages Heard Over WWJ.

are representative of a dozen of the greatest orchestras of the United States, with which they have been connected.

One of the most notable early achievements of the News radio was the discovery of a lost boy and his subsequent return to his home. The lad was Albino Tanner Fleming, 13-year-old adopted son of William Fleming. The boy left home, with St. Louis as his destination, but his foster father succeeded in locating him over the radio, after fruitless communication with the police of many cities for many days. He was found in Toledo. An amateur operator in that city gave the boy's description to the matron of the juvenile detention home, who at once identified one of her charges as the missing boy. A few weeks later this incident was paralleled in almost every detail.

The News then offered Mayor James Couzens, of Detroit, and the state, the co-operation of its transmitting station in the tracking of criminals, the suppression of crime, and recovery of stolen property. This offer has been accepted and Station WWJ now "stands by" for any such service called for.

Special equipment has been installed for receipt and transmission of time signals from the Government station at Arlington, near Washington. These are sent out daily from 11:52 a. m. to 12:00 noon, thereby enabling operators throughout the entire field covered by the News transmitter to synchronize their time pieces with the Government chronometer at Washington.

In addition to broadcasting, The News has sponsored the Detroit Radio Association, an organization which has already done much to stimulate interest in wireless telephony and to disseminate useful information to radio enthusiasts. For several months lectures were given before members, in the studio on Saturdays, by men from the technical department, and these proved exceedingly valuable to amateurs.

A striking example of the radio's potentiality as a disseminator of news was furnished in March, 1922, when a great sleet storm struck down the wires all over lower Michigan and southern Ontario. Papers in the southern part of the state were entirely cut off from the service of the Associated Press, the great news gathering organization, and other agencies on which they depend for their news of the world. Many were able, however, to print their bulletins without interruption, for the news was broadcast by Station WWJ. Amateurs in several cities conveyed the reports to newspapers entitled to them, and others loaned the use of instruments, stenographers transcribing the news for publication.

Since the present enlarged service program was instituted, The News has received letters from Honduras, from Saskatchewan and Alberta and Nova Scotia; from Cuba, the Canal Zone, and Porto Rico; from a lonely ranchman in Wyoming and from scores of other remote places, expressing thanks to The Detroit News for bringing across the great spaces splendid music, first-class theatrical entertainments and rousing and stimulating messages from the leaders of the country's thought. Letters tell also of a mother in Nebraska hearing her son, a minister, preach in Detroit; of a girl in Los Angeles hearing her brother play on the violin at The News' studio.

All this has been extremely gratifying to the publishers and has persuaded them that enhanced public usefulness is the ample justification for the great expenditure which the radio service has entailed.

A curious thing in connection with the broadcasting has been the reaction of stage artists to the undemonstrative bronze device into which they pour their songs and remarks. Frank Tinney refused to believe that he was not the victim of a hoax. He feared he was in reality talking for the sole entertainment of practical jokers in the private room where the microphone of the transmitting apparatus was located, until he heard music relayed back by telephone from Windsor, Ont., across the river. Embarrassment, even acute "stage fright," has been noticed in the case of almost every individual who is accustomed to applause as occasional motive power.

The News on Dec. 18, 1921, commented on this as follows:

"The receiver is not a very appreciative instrument, at least in appearance. One can't tell from the looks of the microphone whether his number is liked or not.

"This was quite baffling to Ernie Ball. He sang one or two of his most popular numbers, heard no applause and finally looked at the telephone in a manner that registered blind rage. And then he stuck out his tongue at the instrument, which seemed to relieve his feelings a lot, for he swung immediately into another selection."

The growth of the Detroit News station has been along two lines—a development of equipment and a development in social service. It was on the first of February, 1922, that the installation of the present powerful instruments for a continent-wide service was completed. They were built to the special order of The News.

Under the very worst of conditions—such as a severe electric storm—the station will transmit 100 miles and it has been known to send 4,300 miles on a still winter's night. On the whole, the winter is a better time for successful broadcasting than the summer, for then the atmosphere is less liable to static disturbances.

Amateurs who "listen in" on the News program are provided with either of two sorts of receiving sets. These are the tube detector set, which will receive at great distances, and the crystal detector set, whose range is not so great. The crystal sets have been known to accomplish successful results at a distance of several hundred miles, but most small sets have a very limited scope and the amateur must not expect the ordinary crystal set to operate at anything over 75 miles. Some sets are now being manufactured, tuned permanently to

The Radio Staff of The Detroit News

Upper row: Edwin G. Boyes, Walter R. Hoffman and Keith Bernand, engineer-operators; Genevieve Champagne, secretary; E. Lloyd Tyson, assistant program director; Elton M. Plant, reporter. Lower row: Charles D. Kelley, department editor and supervisor; Howard E. Campbell, chief radio engineer; William F. Holliday, program director; G. Marshall Witchell, reporter.

the News station, with fixed detectors, and guaranteed
to receive programs clearly from 10 to 20 miles.

Of late The News has devoted many of its columns to
radio activities, satisfying an intense interest in the new
science throughout its field of circulation, through the
printed page as well as the ether. The radio writers
furnish the reader with a great deal of diversified information of scientific value, in addition to "human-in-
terest" news. This radio department is a daily feature,
and for the Sunday edition a weekly survey of the radio
situation is prepared, dealing more elaborately with the
subject and devoting considerable space to simplified
scientific discussions of broadcasting and receiving.

WWJ's programs for the ensuing week are printed
each Sunday, and every day during the week The News
carries the programs for two days in advance.

The editorial staff of The Detroit News contributes
both meat and sauce to the varied programs of WWJ,
and these contributions are printed daily in the newspaper.

Perhaps the most popular feature of the programs, at
least until the organization of The Detroit News Orchestra, was the Town Crier. At first he held to the tradi-
tions of bellmen, and gave a nightly digest of the day's
news, with running comment. His whimsicality was so
appealing that fancy ultimately took precedence over fact.
The anonymity which at first characterized the Town
Crier could not be maintained. He is Al Weeks, dramatic critic of The News, and, betimes, dramatist and
actor as well as wag.

The Town Crier's accoutrements have an interesting
past. One bell that sounds over the radio was used by
the Toronto schoolmaster, Alexander Muir, beloved by
Canadians as the author of their national anthem, "The
Maple Leaf Forever." Another, still bearing the mud
and stains of an Argonne battlefield, served a French
town crier in the days before the war.

Others whose offerings over the radio are highly
valued are Miss Florence Davies, who chats helpfully

with housewives each morning, and Leland Bell, who gives courses in physical training for women.

The ever increasing radio family of WWJ may be assured The Detroit News will keep abreast of invention and thought to the end that the public may profit to the utmost during the future growth of this science.

The Detroit News Orchestra

THE Detroit News Orchestra, the first radio orchestra ever organized, is a 16-piece symphonic ensemble, all of whose members have achieved distinction with the Detroit Symphony Orchestra under the baton of the great pianist-conductor, Ossip Gabrilowitsch, or with other famous musical organizations. Each is an accomplished soloist who will contribute to the quality of the radio programs of The Detroit News by individual numbers, as well as in concert.

This "little symphony" will serve those who listen in on WWJ nightly, and will, in addition, be loaned from time to time in the interests of musical appreciation to churches, educational institutions and other non-commercial organizations for recitals. For all of its superlative capacity in any realm of music, the orchestra will not be of the ultra-classical type, nor will it scorn the harmonies and melodies which the general public fondly cherishes.

Following is the personnel of the ensemble:

Otto E. Krueger, conductor; organizer of many musical ensembles; flautist with Detroit Symphony Orchestra for the past five years.

Maurice Warner, concertmeister; member of New York Symphony Orchestra on European tour, and soloist throughout United States and Canada; first violin, Detroit Symphony Orchestra.

Herman Goldstein, first violin; soloist and member of Boston and Detroit Symphony Orchestras.

LeRoy Hancock, first violin; member of Cincinnati, St. Paul and Detroit Symphony Orchestras.

Armand Hebert, second violin; concert soloist and member of Seattle Symphony Orchestra.

V. P. Coffey, viola and piano; composer and member of Cincinnati, Philadelphia and Detroit Symphony Orchestras.

Frederick Broeder, cello; member of Cincinnati, St. Paul and Detroit Symphony Orchestras and Russian Ballet Orchestra.

Eugene W. Braunsdorf, bass; soloist with many concert organizations; member of Detroit Symphony Orchestra for five years.

Thomas J. Byrne, oboe; soloist with many concert organizations; member of Detroit Symphony Orchestra for five years.

R. M. Arey, clarinet; Boston Festival Orchestra, Boston Opera Company, soloist with Boston Municipal Orchestra; solo-clarinetist of Detroit Symphony Orchestra.

Vincenzo Pezzi, bassoon; member of St. Paul, Minneapolis and Detroit Symphony Orchestras.

Albert Stagliamo, French horn; soloist with many concert organizations; solo-hornist of Detroit Symphony Orchestra.

Edward Clarke, French horn; with many concert organizations.

Floyd O'Hara, trumpet; concert soloist; member of Detroit Symphony Orchestra for five years.

Max Smith, trombone; concert soloist; member of Cincinnati Symphony Orchestra and solo-trombonist of Detroit Symphony Orchestra.

Arthur Cooper, xylophone and percussion instruments; concert soloist; first percussionist of Detroit Symphony Orchestra.

Executive Offices of WWJ

Broadcasting Equipment of WWJ

THE DETROIT NEWS Radio Broadcasting Station (WWJ) has apparatus as follows, made by the Western Electric Company:

1. A set of microphones of special design (double carbon button) to transform sound into electrical energy.

2. A speech-current amplifier (Type A) to increase the power of the microphone-output ready for transmitter.

3. A radio transmitter (Type 1-A) including a 50-watt vacuum tube speech input amplifier and four 250-watt vacuum tubes, two as oscillators and two as modulators—the whole to further the energy and transfer it to the antenna.

4. A 5½ H. P. motor, driving a 1600-volt, 1.8-kilowatt plate current-generator and a 16-volt, 615-watt filament current-generator, providing power for transmitter's tubes.

5. A series of dry cells of 130 volts and storage battery of 12 volts providing power for tubes of the speech-current amplifier.

6. A monitoring loud speaker (196 W) for regulating performers and amplifiers.

7. An antenna of 4 wires each 250 feet (T type).

Normally this transmitter has an input to its antenna of 500 watts, giving about 7 amperes to the entertainment and news waves of 360 meters, and about 11 amperes to the weather waves of 485 meters for Government reports.

Broadcasting Schedule of WWJ

IN MAY, 1922, the following schedule for WWJ—The Detroit News—was established, subject, of course, to alteration under changing Governmental regulations:

Week Days.

9:30 to 9:40 a. m.—Hints to housewives.
9:40 to 10:15 a. m.—Music reproduced.
10:15 to 10:30 a. m.—Weather report.
11:52 a. m. to 12:00 noon—U. S. Naval Observatory time
signals.
12:05 to 12:45 p. m.—Music reproduced.
3:30 to 3:40 p. m.—Weather report.
3:40 to 4:15 p. m.—Market quotations.
5:00 to 6:00 p. m.—Complete base ball scores, additional
markets, and special features as announced.

Week Nights.

For alternate weeks, including the weeks of May 28,
June 11, June 25, July 9, and continuing thus:
   7:00 to 8:30 p. m.—Entertainment and edification by
   musicians and speakers.
For alternate weeks, including the weeks of May 21,
June 4, June 18, July 2, and continuing thus:
   8:30 to 10:00 p. m.—Entertainment and edification by
   musicians and speakers.

Sundays.

Alternate Sundays, including May 28, June 11, June
28, July 9, etc.:
   9:30 a. m. to 2:00 p. m.—Church services and special
   programs.
   4:00 p. m. to 6:00 p. m.—Special programs.
Alternate Sundays, including June 4, June 18, July 2,
etc.:
   2:00 to 4:00 p. m.—Special programs.
   6:00 to 10:00 p. m.—Church services and special programs.

   Note: Weather and all other Government reports are
broadcast on 485 meters; everything else is on 360
meters. All special programs are announced, both as
to time and character, in the columns of The News, and
by radiotelephone.

Behind the Scenes

THE public, grown familiar with at least the superficial aspects of radio-reception, is still largely in ignorance of the conditions under which broadcasting is accomplished. From the standpoint of the performer, sending is as simple as it is, from the standpoint of the scientist, complex. The very informality of broadcasting, in contrast with its incalculable importance, startles and embarrasses artist and speaker.

Those who wish to appear on WWJ's program make their first acquaintance with the program director or his assistant in the "booking office," which is a part of the executive suite—and one of nine rooms devoted to the radio department. If their merits are unknown to the director, entertainers are given an opportunity to reveal their talent in the studios, under conditions prevailing during transmisson. If successful, they are received the evening of their scheduled appearance in the auditorium, a spacious room between the operating rooms and the studios, and await their turn, with others on the program.

The auditorium is equipped with a receiving set and loud-speaker, so that artists and speakers may hear the program just as it is being heard everywhere within WWJ's range. This receiving set is so equipped and adjusted as to approximate all conditions of reception at a distance of five miles; and while it furnishes diversion for waiting performers, it also is a guide to the engineer-operators in the adjustment of the transmitting apparatus, and the giving of instructions to entertainers. The auditorium also contains a blackboard bearing the program, and advising each "number" of his place on the "bill."

The program director and his assistant act as stage managers. They call the artists in turn to the adjoining main studio, a room 26 by 28 feet, especially prepared

Operating Room of WWJ

Showing transmitter (rear left), power panel (rear center), speech-current amplifier (right), and microphone (the circular instrument with cord attached).

from a standpoint of acoustics. This room has been made echo-proof through the use of specially constructed walls and ceilings, padded with felt two inches thick. Curtains of friar's cloth are hung over doorways, windows and walls, the further to deaden all sounds save those which are to be transmitted. The floor is, for the same reason, covered with a thick blue carpet.

The equipment of the main studio includes two grand pianos, an upright piano, four or five phonographs of various makes, music stands and cabinets, a reading desk and sundry furnishings for comfort and convenience.

Inconspicuous, except to the entertainers, is a box-like, electrically operated device somewhat resembling the electric enunciators used in hospitals. It is connected with the radio engineer's desk, and is his means of communication with the entertainer. The face of this indicator bears such legends as "Farther from the phone," "Louder," "Softer," and "Stop." The operator can touch a button, making a light glow behind whatever legend he wishes to signal for the guidance of musician or speaker.

A duplicate of this device is in a smaller studio, likewise sound deadened, and reserved for speakers and for the transmission of news. This studio is furnished with a reading table, reading lamp, deep leather chair, carafe and other comforts.

WWJ learned early the performer's need of privacy; and when he enters the studios, he is alone except for the announcer. Occasionally this very privacy is distressing to artists who need a visible and responsive audience as a stimulus; but its advantages overweigh this objection, and embarrassment speedily passes. Occasionally an entertainer comes dressed to please the most fastidious eye in the unseeing audience; but the more experienced are aware of the utter informality of the occasion, and conduct themselves as in rehearsal. It it no uncommon thing for a distinguished artist, such as John Steele, operatic star, to doff coat, waistcoat, collar and necktie before singing.

In each of the studios there is the all-essential microphone. The newer type of instrument looks much like
a bronze mantel clock, except that it has no dial; and it is
approximately six inches in diameter. It has no horn or
other flaring contrivance; but it catches all sounds directed toward it and changes them to electrical vibrations.
From each microphone, three wires run to the operating
room where the electrical vibrations are increased in
strength and then impressed on the transmitter, which
projects them through the ether in the form of electro-
magnetic waves, on errands of intelligence and entertainment. Never more than one microphone is used at a
time.

The electrical processes by which this modern miracle
in transformation and transmission is accomplished are,
roughly, as follows:

When the sound waves from the throat or from musical instruments strike the diaphragm of the microphone,
they cause it to vibrate. The vibrations alternately com-
press and release a small column of carbon particles, thus
varying what is known as contact resistance, through
the column.

The resistance of the carbon particles is high when
the diaphragm is not in motion, and therefore very little
current flows through the speech-current circuit. But
as soon as the sound waves strike the diaphragm, the resistance of this carbon column is varied, slowly for low-
pitched notes, and more rapidly for the high-pitched.

The pulsations of electrical current are allowed to pass
through the speech-current circuit in the exact form of
the vibrations of the speech energy. At the other end of
the circuit these minute pulsations of electrical energy
are made to control the action of a series of vacuum
tubes which greatly amplify, or increase, the amount of
this current, and still preserve its true form for reproduction of sound vibrations. This part of the circuit is
called the speech-current amplifier.

From here the current goes through another circuit

into the radiophone transmitter, where the speech-current is once more amplified by actuating a small power tube before being finally impressed upon big modulation tubes. By this time the speech-current pulsations from the microphone have been "stepped up," or amplified, hundreds of thousands of times, but without altering the relative form of the vibrations.

At this point the speech-current is used to change the form of the continuous electrical oscillations in the radio transmitter so that very powerful pulsations are sent into the aerial, and sent out therefrom in all directions with the speed of light (186,000 miles a second), but still in such form as faithfully to reproduce speech, music or other sounds conveyed to the little microphone. It is the business of receiving sets to convert the electromagnetic waves, through crystal or vacuum tube and telephone receiver, back into sound waves.

Visitors to The Detroit News Building are shown behind the scenes in this as well as other departments by a guide, at 1 and 3 p. m. each week day. Persons seeking technical information are welcome at the department from 9 a. m. to 5 p. m., or may address inquiries to the Radio Editor.

Interior of Power Panel (Left) and Transmitter.

The Farmer and WWJ

IT is the prophecy of farm leaders everywhere that in agriculture more than in any other industry, the radiophone will reach its greatest usefulness to the nation.

There even have been prophets to place radio ahead of the rural mail, the telephone or the automobile as an agency for bettering social conditions and making the farm a magnet to attract and hold the interest of the coming generation. These herald the new voices of the air as an especial godsend to the isolated farm, as was the wireless telegraph previously a godsend to the sea.

The radiophone has arrived as a dramatic climax to a series of improvements destined to equalize the social advantages of town and country through better means of communication and entertainment. When it is realized that 32,000,000 persons live upon farms in the United States, the opportunity for this service is apparent.

While the United States Department of Agriculture had, since December 15, 1920, been using the radiotelegraph for broadcasting market reports, the radiotelephone was not much in use for that purpose until 1922. The Government market system the first year included mail radiotelegraph stations at Washington, Cincinnati, St. Louis, Omaha, North Platte, Neb., Rock Springs, Wyo., and Elko and Reno, Nev., each of them having a radius of 300 miles.

The difficulty with this broadcasting by the Government was that, being done by radiotelegraph, the signals could be read only by persons proficient in copying telegraph code. The radiotelephone, on the other hand, enables any farmer equipped with a moderate priced receiver to take advantage of the service.

It was to give the farmers and other business men of the upper and lower peninsulas of Michigan, Ontario and adjoining states, this better and more practical service that The Detroit News early in 1922 began a daily broadcast of market quotations by radiophone, embracing the following: The close of the Detroit Stock Exchange, the Michigan Central livestock reports, quotations on livestock from Chicago and other points, the close of the Chicago and other grain markets, Wall Street's closing prices and the New York money market.

Joined with this were Government weather forecasts, market quotations, crop estimates and reports on the spread of harmful insects and plant and animal epidemics.

The service was given enthusiastic reception by farmers and business men who then had receiving sets. Letters of approval that continue to come to Station WWJ, especially from farmers, show the important part this station is to play in the spread of economic information of untold value in the raising and marketing of crops on a more businesslike basis.

Of no less importance to the rural sections is The News' program of university extension. Professors from both the University of Michigan and the Michigan Agricultural College have already given addresses which have been "attended by radio" over state and nation. The U. of M. professors have, of course, spoken on matters of general educational interest, but those from M. A. C. have lectured and will continue to lecture on subjects of particular interest and value to the farmers.

David M. Friday, president of M. A. C., arranged with The News to furnish some member of his staff once every week, except in the vacation period, to deliver an address on seasonable and important agricultural subjects in the News studio. President Friday suggested at the start that the talks be given on Saturday evenings; for that is the time when the members of the grange ordinarily hold their meetings, or when farmers gather in the nearest town. Receiving sets owned by granges or stores therefore could distribute intelligence to groups. It was undersood, of course, that as receiving sets became more numerous in the rural districts, and as the system expanded, the time, wave-length and character of the various services of the radio would be subject to changes, these to be announced from time to time in The News or from Station WWJ.

The agricultural extension lectures began on the evening of Saturday, April 8, 1922. Prof. H. C. Rather, extension specialist of the Michigan Agricultural College, and secretary-treasurer of the Michigan Crop Improvement Association, spoke on quality seeds as a means toward quality crops, and told his invisible audience how the state of Michigan had arranged, through co-operation between the college and the association, to provide the farmers of the state with seeds of known and demonstrated excellence.

It is the opinion of President Friday that the radio is bound to work out a closer union between the farmers of Michigan and the inhabitants of the cities and towns, and to mean much in the promotion of a sympathetic solidarity in the state's citizenry.

Among the earliest radio enthusiasts was Albert B. Cook of Shiawassee County, master of the Michigan State Grange, whose son installed in their house a home-made set at a cost of $20. Mr. Cook at once proclaimed this as the modern Aladdin's lamp, because of the diversity of its wonders.

"We have here," said he, "a first-class source of information on prices and conditions for all kinds of farming whether cereal, dairying, special or general crops. It will bring to us with the speed of lightning warnings of swarming insects, agricultural epidemics and destructive invasions. It will keep our eyes open for changes in the weather—all of this sufficiently in advance to save untold thousands of dollars to the farmers, once full advantage is taken of the system.

"But further than that, it brings to our firesides, instructive and culturing entertainment, music, drolleries —a divertisement we had not before on the farm."

The mountain refused to go to Mahomet but the city is in a fair way to be taken to the farmer without the necessity of his stepping outside the sitting room of his home.

A Worthy Habitation

THOSE relatively few Detroiters who remember the day, August 23, 1873, when James Edmund Scripps took the first copy of The News from the press, were not surprised when on its forty-seventh birthday, the paper became the journalistic pioneer in broadcasting intelligence and entertainment by radiotelephone. That innovation was in line with the determination of its founder and his successors in the administration of the newspaper to keep it ever foremost in its field, and in the vanguard of progressivism in the nation's journalism. "Always in the lead" has been, from the first, its realized motto in editorial enterprise, social service and business acumen.

In its first decade, The Detroit News burdened the soul of its founder with economic problems; for its instant success surpassed all expectation, and Mr. Scripps was hard pressed for funds with which to produce his publication in such quantity as would satisfy the demand. In time, financial shortages ceased to harass the publisher, but The Detroit News has never, in its 49 years of existence, known a span of five years when it could count its plant adequate to meet its every need. And this, despite careful planning. Neither the most visionary nor the astutest of the executives could possibly have foreseen with any certainty either the growth of the city and state which the paper has served, the ever-increasing respect and relish of the public for its columns, or the additions to the functions of the press, such, for example, as radiotelephone broadcasting.

When James E. Scripps laid the corner stone of the little one-story brick addition to a frame house, which constituted the first home of The News, he could not even vaguely have conceived of the paper's ultimate occupancy of the largest and finest newspaper manufactory in the world; and within a decade of his death. And when, in 1900, he came readily to the assistance of Mich-

igan's radio pioneer, Thomas E. Clark, with an endow-
ment of a thousand dollars for necessary researches, he
most certainly did not foresee that within the lifetime of
his venerable widow, The Detroit News would give over
to radio 3003 square feet of floor space—more, indeed,
than the entire plant needed for the four-page newspaper of the early seventies.

The magnificent stone and steel structure into which
The Detroit News moved in 1917 was the product of a
quarter of a century of incessant planning. It occupied a
full half block, covering the historic homestead of Zach-
ariah Chandler, most famous of Michigan's senators, and
extending from Fort to Lafayette on Second Boulevard,
a distance of 280 feet, with a frontage of 150 feet on each
of the first named thoroughfares. It was thought ample
to meet the needs of the publication for years to come;
yet within a twelve-month additions were found necessary. The third, and eventually the fourth quarter of the
block were acquired, and now The News occupies the
entire square.

The additions extended not merely to this space, on
which a vast paper warehouse and garage were constructed, but touched even the main building, on which
was superimposed a fourth story, behind the decorative
parapet; and in a portion of the added floor the now famous radio station, WWJ, is housed. This department includes a suite of executive offices, the technical laboratory, operating room, the reception room for artists
and the public, the studio whence musical numbers are
broadcast, and another for individuals delivering addresses to the "radio family" of The News.

Each year ten thousand persons are shown through
The Detroit News Building, many of whom are publishers with a deep professional interest in its design and
equipment. Journalists of more than a score of foreign
countries, and from every continent, have inspected the
plant; and many at home and abroad have made it the
basis for new buildings, in some instances practically
replicas on a smaller scale. But of course the vast ma-

Laboratory of WWJ. Showing Motor and Generator.

jority of the visitors are of the populace which makes up the clientele of the paper, and they are actuated not by professional interests but human curiosity with regard to the press as a great social institution, and by a deep regard for the fine and the beautiful, as represented in the building's architecture, decoration and equipment.

But while nobility of design and conforming dignity of furnishings are notable features of the building, the aim and achievement of the publishers and the architect, Mr. Albert Kahn, were a combination of such qualities as would result in a building expressing the semi-public functions of the press and at the same time demonstrating modern factory efficiency principles. Neither good taste nor sound practice in plant construction was sacrificed, one for the other. In the end there was realized an edifice which is a distinct contribution to American architecture, and known as such the world over. It frankly acknowledges its indebtedness to the past, not merely in its appropriation and adaptation of modern and medieval European architectural elements, but in the carved stone figures of Gutenberg, Caxton, Plantin and Greeley, fathers of journalism, which adorn the parapet; and in the colophons, or printers' marks, which are engraved on decorative shields on the exterior, in recognition of the master craftsmen of another age.

The inscriptions on the parapet, of which Prof. F. N. Scott, of the University of Michigan, is the author, are an added feature of the exterior. They express the ideal of the newspaper housed therein and the goal toward which it strives:

Mirror of the Public Mind . . Interpreter of the Public Intent . . Troubler of the Public Conscience

Reflector of Every Human Interest . . Friend of Every Righteous Cause . . Encourager of Every Generous Act

Bearer of Intelligence . . Dispeller of Ignorance and Predjuice . . A Light Shining into All Dark Places

Promoter of Civic Welfare and Civic
Pride . . Bond of Civic Unity . . Protector
of Civic Rights

Scourge of Evil Doers . . Exposer of Secret
Iniquities . . Unrelenting Foe of Privilege and
·Corruption

Voice of the Lowly and Oppressed . . Ad-
vocate of the Friendless . . Righter of Public
and Private Wrongs

Chronicler of Facts . . Sifter of Rumors and
Opinions . . Minister of the Truth That Makes
Men Free.

Reporter of the New . . Remembrancer of
the Old and Tried . . Herald of What Is to
Come

Defender of Civil Liberty . . Strengthener
of Loyalty . . Pillar and Stay of Democratic
Government

Upbuilder of the Home . . Nourisher of the
Community Spirit . . Art, Letters, and Science
of the Common People

The decorations in the first and second floor lobbies
are of a modified Renaissance character; and the former
is made particularly impressive by the wrought steel
vestibule at the entrance, the steel grilles in the tym-
panums at either end, the light fixture suggesting a medieval globe, and the low relief figures representing Government, Commerce, History and Philosophy, in broad-
sweeping lunettes. These features are rivaled only by
the stained glass windows in The News' private library,
as masterpieces in modern craftsmanship. Lesser points
of interest for their richness are the various executive and
administrative offices, wainscoted in modified Eliza-
bethan style; the library, with its arched and modeled
ceiling and its deep alcoves with colorful and learning-
laden shelves; and the art department, with its heavily
beamed ceiling and its booths for individual artists, having an air of cloister cells.

Deep as is the interest of guests in such elements of

beauty, those things which give greatest pause are the various mechanical divisions of the paper where are wrought the wonders which result in the speedy dissemination of knowledge to a waiting world.

In the composing room, spacious and airy, 144 men do miracles with well-nigh human type-setting machines and their glistening product. Each of these machines, of which there are two-score, runs night and day and is capable of the output of five or six hand compositors. The pages of type, when assembled, move to the stereotyping department, where they are duplicated by an elaborate and fascinating process. Matrices of damp, blotter-like paper are imposed upon the pages of type and made to take a perfect impression of the type- and cut-faces by being subjected to enormous pressure. Then they are baked dry while still under pressure, and become the molds from which semi-cylindrical plates of type-metal, in exact duplication of the original forms of type, except for shape, are cast by ponderous machines. The plates fit the cylinders of the presses and make possible the simultaneous printing of identical newspapers on broad ribbons of paper. Workmen in this department handle 75 tons of metal daily.

The presses which print the complete daily editions and the black and white sections of the Sunday newspaper, form a battery of thirty synchronized units, to which six more now under construction will shortly be added. They are 193 feet 2 inches long, over all, and have a capacity of 504,000 complete 16-page papers, printed, cut, folded, counted and delivered to the shipping room every hour. These voracious machines consume nearly 140 rolls, each containing six miles of paper, every day. Last year's total approximated 300,000 miles of paper of a standard width of 70 inches. The immediate storage pier, 147 feet long and 50 feet wide, is emptied of its burden of rolls in a day and a half; and the paper warehouse has a capacity of 12,000 rolls, or 72,000 miles of paper. Each day's output of The News involves the consumption of 3,300 pounds of ink.

The Main Lobby of The Detroit News Building.

Here the News of the Day Is Assembled.

The News Library Contains 18,000 Volumes.

World's Records for Advertising Lineage Are Set Here.

Two Score Typesetting Machines Serve the Composing Room.

The Stereotypers Handle 75 Tons of Metal Daily.

The Presses Consume 300,000 Miles of Paper Yearly.

A Fleet of 72 Autos Awaits the Press Room's Product.

The Detroit News is the only newspaper in Michigan having a rotogravure department of its own; and the highly technical and involved process of etching the copper cylinders and printing the rotogravure section is one understood by few not engaged in the business—and successfully described to the layman by none. The color press, capable of printing four colors at once and a great variety of shades, works, like the rotogravure presses, at a much lower speed than the big battery devoted to the black and white sections. The color press prints the illustrated magazine section and the colored comics of the Sunday edition of The News simultaneously at the rate of 11,000 an hour.

Those of an electrical turn of mind will be interested to know that the safety automatic control board regulating the operation of the presses includes 62 feet of marble panels of more than head height; and that The News is the only newspaper in the world whose power (entirely electrical) is drawn from a remotely controlled substation within its own walls. Here alternating current at a pressure of 4,600 volts is transformed to direct current.

The art and engraving departments work in close co-operation, and their efficient equipment makes possible on the one hand the rapid development of photographic negatives, and on the other the utmost speed in the production of "cuts." A halftone engraving has been etched and made ready for reproduction of a photograph in the paper in 21 minutes, though no such speed is ordinarily attempted.

The business and editorial offices are humming places of industry and mental application to the numberless problems of journalism; but less spectacularly interesting than mechanical departments, naturally.

Into the editorial department, news and pictures from the ends of the earth come in a never-diminishing torrent, the while the local staff mercilessly inflicts its own product on the harassed "copy-readers." The four greatest news gathering agencies, 15 "feature syndicates" and five leading photographic services supply matter for the paper, in addition to the output of its thousand special correspondents in Michigan and its bureaus operated by members of the editorial staff in Washington, New York, London and Berlin. Sixteen manual telegraph instruments and two automatic, within the building, bring news of the outer world, to which the customary services of the telegraph companies are but a supplement.

A library of 18,000 volumes and a scraparium where are filed 30,000 engravings and data and pictures touching 80,000 subjects or persons, are invaluable adjuncts to the editorial department.

The business office does not, to the casual onlooker, reveal the myriad threads by which it directs the efforts, not merely of nine hundred employes within the walls of The News, but 5,000 newsboys in Detroit, 3,000 more in the state, 1,450 city news stands, 101 city supply stations 950 state agents, and the fleet of 72 automobiles employed in distributing the papers, handling raw materials and doing the unnumbered other tasks of a metropolitan newspaper. Four long rows of telephones in a sound-deadened room, with industrious clerks attending them, indicate the inner connection with the 458 stations in the city where classified advertising is left for The News. These telephones are a part of the 167 connected with 70 trunk lines, which maintain communication with the public. For interdepartmental communication, there is an automatic private telephone system, such as Detroit is promised for general use in the near future.

As a result of the zeal of this department in presenting the merits of the paper to the business world, The News has with astonishing consistency set world's records for total advertising lineage.

It goes without saying that, in providing nearly 275,000 square feet of floor space for the multiple tasks of newspaper production, The News has made generous provision for the comfort and convenience of its employes, in addition to the necessary efficient working quarters. There is an admirably equipped cafe; a hos-

pital without a superior in attractiveness or complete-
ness of equipment for industrial casualties; a conference
and reading room, where lectures, concerts, motion pic-
ture showings, dances and other entertainments may be
held. The air in the building is washed. Refrigerated
water is supplied all departments. The rapid growth of
the paper, and the increasing demands for space have
obliterated the tennis court which once occupied a portion of the roof, and a few other features of a recreative
character, for the time being.

The best thought of the various staffs of The News is
constantly directed toward the needs of the future. What
this will mean in further extensions of the remarkable
plant of the newspaper, only the future can tell. They
will, if past experience count for anything, be as remarkable as those herein outlined.

"This Is WWJ—The Detroit News."

The Genesis of Radiotelephony

R ADIO TELEPHONY, like all attempts to utilize the mysterious forces of the universe, is largely a matter of theory and experiment. We are dealing with invisible things. The various phenomena that we are able to produce are merely the effects of certain manipulations. Electricity, magnetism, radio-activity and even such familiar things as light, heat and the manifestation of color are only the effects of certain disturbances which we have learned how to accomplish in the invisible elemental substance or substances which surround us.

Theories regarding these phenomena have undergone many changes. For many years electricity was regarded as a fluid. For a time it was regarded as two fluids. As an inheritance of these discarded theories mechanical electricians still often style electric current as "juice" because, by providing suitable conductors it can be made to flow in a particular direction and along a certain path. When one asks why it is that by merely swinging a coil of copper wire through the field of a powerful magnet a current of electricity will pass through the wire in one direction as the wire approaches the center of the magnetic influence and why the current is reversed and flows through the coil in the opposite direction as it moves away from that center of attraction, the answer leads us into the very heart of the theory of electricity.

In elementary physics we learn of the "molecular theory of magnetism." The molecules of ferrous metal are, each and every one, separate and distinct permanent magnets—each with a north and south pole, like a tiny earth. Each pole has an attraction for its opposite pole (likes repel, unlikes attract, you know) and all these magnets give off lines of force in little circles called magnetism, due to that attraction of likes for unlikes.

When a bar of iron or steel is said to be unmagnetized, this condition exists in the metal: The little mole-

"Hear ye! Hear ye!! Hear ye!!!

The Town Crier, whose whimsical approach to life is an ever popular feature of WWJ programs, could not long remain anonymous. He is Al Weeks, dramatic critic of The Detroit News, and well known as a humorist, dramatist and actor.

cule-magnets are now pointing their north poles in
various directions. Each magnet, or group of magnets,
in its own little sphere of influence, has its own tiny
circles of force so small that they are entirely within the
metal, the result being that no influence extends outside
the bar.

But when we bring the bar under a sufficiently strong
influence of some other magnetized body, all these little
magnets in the metal rearrange themselves to point their
north poles in the same direction, all the south poles, of
course, pointing the opposite way. This causes the circles or lines of force to be given a common direction,
with the result that they join forces, making large con-
centric circles—now large and strong enough to extend
outside the bar a little way—influencing anything that
comes near the metal within the field of those unseen
lines of force. Then do we say the bar of metal has been
magnetized.

Now, when that copper wire is waved or otherwise
put in motion near this bar, cutting across those unseen
lines of force outside the metal, something takes place in
the copper wire. This is the romance of the atom: There
are in the copper subdivisions of atoms called electrons
and co-electrons or ions, each kind having affinity for the
other kind, and all wedded in pairs—an electron for each
ion.

But the motion of the wire in that magnetic field
causes the couples to be cast asunder. The magnetic influence sends the ions in one direction to the outside of
the field of force, and the electrons in the opposite direction. When the copper wire is a circuit, one kind goes
hurrying down along that circuit—an easy path for them
—traveling however far—each positive male ion trying
to find and wed a negative female electron—each particle
trying to find its affinity. The great stress of these affinity particles in this action we call—electricity!

This movement of the ions and electrons in a circuit
constitutes what is called electric current. When we
manipulate the copper wire so as to have all of the ions

travel the same way constantly and all the electrons travel an opposite way constantly, we call it direct current. When all of the ions go for a short time in one direction and find and wed their affinities, and then the next bunch of them goes for the same space of time in the other direction to find and wed, we call it alternating current.

The creation of current in this way—moving the wire in the magnetic field—is called generation. Outside mechanical force is of course necessary to keep the wire in motion. Induction, on the other hand, is the transfer or taking up of magnetism or electricity from one body to another in its presence, or from one circuit to another nearby, without the necessity of their being in actual contact with each other. A machine for generating is a generator; and a common apparatus for induction is known as an induction coil.

Magnetic influence has been known for a long time, but it was not until the Nineteenth Century was well advanced that the discovery was put to practical use for the generation of electric current. It was not until 1886 that Heinrich Hertz, a student under von Helmholtz, made the startling discovery that the discharge of an electric spark in the atmosphere would set up a wave motion which would be propagated in all directions, and that some of the energy of this wave could be taken up on a coil of wire at some distance.

This was the real beginning of radio development. What remained to be done was to discover how far these waves would travel and to devise instruments which would be capable of absorbing their energy and then amplifying it and translating it into sound. Hertz demonstrated that such waves could be reflected, refracted, or bent out of their regular course, diffracted, or broken up; and also they could be polarized. With the knowledge of these properties in hand the way was opened for radio development. This discovery was published to the world at large in 1887.

Augusto Righi, physicist of the University of Bologna,

began experimenting with Hertzian waves. One of his students was a young man, son of an Italian father and an Irish mother, named Guglielmo Marconi. Marconi concentrated his attention upon radio experiments with such striking success that in 1897 the Marconi Wireless Telegraph Company was organized in Great Britain. Marconi had failed to interest the Italian government in this promotion.

In much the same way that the electro-magnetic telegraph eventually led to the invention of the telephone, so Marconi's experiments and successes with radio-telegraphy led to the production of the wireless telephone or radiophone service. In the early 1870's Elisha Gray constructed a set of magnetic buzzers which would give all the tones of the musical scale. By connecting this device in a telegraph circuit he found that a tune played upon this instrument would be repeated by telegraph sounders within the circuit, quite as well as would the ordinary click of the telegraph sending key.

The human ear, like the human eye, is an imperfect instrument in the average person. Some persons can distinguish qualities in vibrations that are inaudible to others. Likewise some ears have a very fine definition for tunes that are fractional gradations of the ordinary musical scale.

Theoretically at least, the lowest number of vibrations per second that produces a tone of the lowest pitch is about 14, but this tone is only a jarring effect and not at all musical. It is fairly represented by the sound produced by the largest stopped organ pipe. As the number of vibrations per second increases the pitch rises and the highest possible pitch is produced by vibrations between 20,000 and 21,000 per second. For musical purposes the range of vibrations is usually between 40 and 4,000 and many ears fail to record even these modest extremes. Some individuals are tone deaf and pitch deaf, just as others are color blind, victims of astigmatism, or far-sighted or near-sighted. The ear is by far the most complex and the most delicate of all the organs of the human body.

The Detroit News Orchestra

In wire transmission Prof. Gray demonstrated that very rapid oscillations could be transmitted by telegraph as well as the slow clicks of the key. The telephone carried this principle into effect by transmitting the vibrations of the human voice acting upon a thin diaphragm. It was perfectly natural, then, that workers and experimenters in radio should work to the logical conclusion that radio transmissions would carry the tones of a voice or of a musical instrument quite as surely as it would carry the snap of the electric spark. All these phenomena are due, according to present theory, to the agitation of the ether and electrons and co-electrons— for simplicity let's call them all electrons—which prevade not only the atmosphere but all substances and all space and which by their massed formation make of the universe a unit comparable to an illimitable ocean with no bounds to either its length, breadth or depth.

Wireless telegraph and wireless telephone operation merely consist in a discreet agitation of this illimitable element into waves of controlled length. These waves are presumed to go outward in all directions and to immeasurable distances. The sending of the waves or imparting of the vibrations to this body of matter is a relatively simple achievement. The main difficulty lies in the invention of sensitive receiving instruments which will detect them, react to them perceptibly and which will transform them from silence into sound.

The invisible ether and its inclosed flood of electrons is so tenuous a body that it exists and moves independent of the atmosphere, which is in comparison like an open grate or screen through which the electrons with their surrounding envelopes of ether flow at a speed of 184,000 to 186,000 miles per second. When anything moves at such a rate it is difficult to time it with a stop watch. It requires very delicate optical apparatus and experiment to demonstrate the velocity of light, electric current and electron movement, which are all different manifestations of the same thing. Sound travels slowly, as every one can observe by watching the steam emerge from the whistle of a boat on the lakes and noting the

time it takes for the sound of the whistle to reach the
ear. The transmission speed of the air for sound is a
little more than 1,100 feet per second. Water is a little
quicker medium, because it is denser. If the ear is held
near the end of an iron bar 100 feet long while some one
strikes the other end with a hammer two distinct sounds
of the blow are heard, the first, through the mass of the
iron, the second, after an interval, through the air.

The mere fact then that radio transmission of the
voice or a symphony goes over the country in all directions at the same rate as electricity and light indicates
that the medium of transmission is no ordinary visible
element, but that mysterious body of infinitely small
corpuscles which scientists style the "ether".

The telephone began to come into practical use in
1879. For several years its range of operation was short
and it was subject to violent interferences through induction. Talking across a state was regarded as impossible.
In Detroit conversation frequently had to be suspended
while an electric car passed through the line of communication, for the roar of the car motors drowned all
other sounds. It was not until 1893 or 1894 that long
distance communication by phone was opened up
between Detroit and New York and Chicago. A return
wire circuit did away with ground induction. The old
solid carbon Blake transmitters gave place to better
instruments which made use of granulated carbon.

With these few elementary facts in mind we immediately give rein to our imaginations and begin to specu-
late upon the future development of radio and its ultimate possibilities and applications. The prospect stag-
gers us, because we realize that all the time we are
merely standing upon the threshold of a world of wonders and that we are dealing with an element which only
exists as yet in theory but which is supposed to be the
basic element of which all created things are composed
and to which all created things may be, by some
unknown process, again converted. It is the substance
of all matter and either the substance, the cause or the
medium of all energy.

When a sleet storm smote Lower Michigan in the early spring of 1922, and telephone and telegraph wires everywhere broke under their burden of ice, the radiophone was the salvation of many state newspapers. The Associated Press and other news agencies were offered the use of Station WWJ, and for the first time the press received its state, national and foreign dispatches by radio The illustration shows David J. Wilkie, correspondent of the "A. P.," and clippings from some of the newspapers which availed themselves of the facilities of The News.

How to Make Receiving Sets

ANYONE may make and operate receiving sets by following instructions given herewith. All parts are called by their radio names, but their functions are explained in plain, untechnical words so as to be of interest to all readers whether they plan to buy or build.

Three complete outfits are taken up—an ABC or elementary set, an intermediate set, and an advanced loud-speaking set. The cost of making or assembling is given—ranging from $8 for the first to $60 for the second, and $100 for the third.

The average ranges of the three are: ABC set, normal, 25 miles; exceptional, 250 miles. Intermediate set, normal, 100 miles; exceptional, 750 miles. Advanced set, normal, 150 miles; exceptional, 1,500 miles.

"Normal range" refers to the distance of entirely successful reception of Detroit News broadcasts when a receiving set is properly operated under average conditions. Even under unfavorable conditions, broadcasts may still be heard beyond normal range, but at some cost in strength or quality.

Between the given "normal range" and the "exceptional range"—even beyond—is a broad field for the amateur to explore; and the thousands of letters received by WWJ demonstrate that the entire North American continent is within the scope of this station.

In the summer conditions for sending are often unfavorable, due chiefly to static interference. Conversely, in winter conditions are especially favorable for transmission and reception, and the range is often triple or even quadruple that in summer time. Variations in receiving may be due to many conditions, some within and some beyond the power of the recipient to alter.

The Elementary Set

THE SIMPLEST practical receiving apparatus which one may build or assemble at home is called the "crystal detector set." The total cost for materials and parts can be kept within $8.00. With it one may sometimes hear stations hundreds of miles away, but under ordinary circumstances its practical range is about 25 miles.

The parts are: An aerial, a single-slide tuning coil, a crystal detector, a phone, a ground connection, and a lightning protector. This does not include a loudspeaker or a horn, but special and expensive equipment for amplification (increasing the volume of sound) may be added. However two extra phones may be attached to a crystal set at small additional expense, so that from one to three persons may listen in.

One should know at the outset something about each of these parts so that he may recognize them by various names and functions as he goes along.

Aerial—An aerial is also called an antenna. It is a wire, or wires strung in the air or arranged on a frame to catch ether waves. Antennae is the plural of antenna.

Single-slide tuning coil—These ether waves, electro-magnetic, are regulated by various broadcasting stations at the various lengths required by law. The single-slide tuning coil is an instrument to adjust the receiving set to the same length of wave as is used at whatever station you wish to hear. This adjustment is called "tuning in." The tuning coil is copper wire wound around a cylinder in a single layer of close-fitting turns. On the outside of this cylinder running the length of it is a brass rod called the slider rod. On this rod is a brass contact which may be slid along on the rod so as to touch any turn of the wire, thus cutting in to the electric current in the set as many of the turns of wire as will be required to tune in.

Crystal Detector—Electric currents are of various kinds. A crystal detector is a device to change the electric current of the coil into the particular kind we need

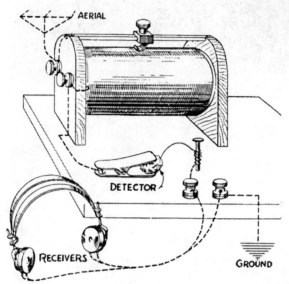

Perspective of a Crystal Detector Set

for hearing purposes. The transmitting station sends out an alternating current. The detector changes it into a direct current, which is the kind required to operate the phone. The main part of this crystal detector is a substance mined out of the earth—commonly a lead ore, chemically known as lead sulphate, commercially as galena. This ore is found in crystalline form, therefore called a crystal. Strange to say, it is the chemical structure of this substance which changes the alternating current to direct, because it allows current to pass through it in only one direction. A crystal detector comprises a small lump of crystal of no particular dimensions—say the size of a pea or a hickory nut—held in place so that the top surface of the lump can be touched at any spot by a fine phosphor-bronze wire, commonly called a "cat-whisker".

Phone—A phone, otherwise known as a receiver or head-set, is an instrument to change electrical vibrations into mechanical vibrations in such a way that they are audible to the human ear. The common telephone receiver is the same thing except that the wireless receiver is more sensitive. The phone figured in this set is a single-ear, or watch-case receiver. A double-ear phone may be procured at extra expense.

Ground-connection—In most electrical work there is a wire for current to go out and another wire for it to come back on to the starting point—a complete circuit. In wireless, the ether serves as one wire and the earth as the return wire—a complete circuit. A ground connection therefore is a method of connecting the receiving set with the earth. This connection is a wire that runs from the set to a metal plate buried in the ground or to a pipe that runs into the ground.

Lightning protector—To prevent the aerial from carrying lightning into the house, a lightning protector should be placed on the aerial wire where it enters the house, and another ground wire from the protector into the ground so that any thunder-bolt would be directed automatically into the earth instead of through the receiving set. A lightning protector is much better than a lightning switch, which therefore need not be described here.

All materials or parts for sets may be bought from electrical or radio supply houses. The following are the principal items to be purchased: 200 feet of No. 14 hard-drawn, bare or insulated copper wire and two or more porcelain cleats, for the antenna; a lightning protector; about 175 feet of No. 22 covered or enameled copper wire, for the coil; three brass binding-posts; a slider rod and slider; a lump of crystal, and about three inches of fine phosphor-bronze wire, for the detector; and a phone.

The simplest form of aerial, and the kind best for receiving purposes, is one continuous, unbroken string of wire, described in two parts; one, the part which is suspended in an elevated, horizontal position near the receiving station, and called the "flat top"; the other part being the end which is brought down to the receiving room, and is called the "lead-in". It is on this lead-in that the lightning protector is placed as described by instructions that come with that device.

The aerial should not be erected near or over any electric power wire. It must be insulated from other wires or cords which are used to suspend it in the air. Insulation is obtained by using porcelain cleats to join the aerial with its supports.

If there is insufficient space on the premises for a single wire about 200 feet long, two or more parallel strands spaced three feet or more apart may be erected, the strands in all totaling the 200 feet. All strands, of course, must be similarly insulated with porcelain cleats; and the lead-in must make a connection with each strand, preferably a soldered connection.

A single-slide tuning coil can be made by winding about 175 feet of No. 22 wire on a rolled-oats box, or paste board tube at least three inches in diameter, and about one foot long.

End pieces, about four inches square, for this tube and a baseboard for it, about 6 by 14 inches, are made of wood. The end pieces are nailed to the baseboard. The wire coil does not touch the baseboard.

Either on the baseboard, or end pieces, are placed the three connection posts, or binding-posts. One post is labeled A for aerial; one is labeled P for phone; the other G for ground.

One end of the coil of wire on the tube leads to the aerial binding-post, to which also is fastened the lead-in from the aerial. The other end of the coil makes no connection but is fastened securely to the tube to prevent unwinding.

The slider rod which carries the slider, which in turn makes contact with the wound wire, is fastened to the two end pieces by screws or staples. And so that the slider may make contact with each turn of the coil, the enamel or insulation on the wire is removed with a piece of sandpaper along the path traveled by the slider.

To make the simplest form of crystal detector, a thin piece of copper sheet is cut about 1 or 1¼ inches square. The corners are bent up to form grips for the lump of crystal. A nail or screw through the center of this piece of copper fastens it to the base board. Before the nail is driven down tight, the end of a small piece of copper wire is fastened around the nail underneath the copper plate. The other end of this piece of wire is fastened to the slider rod. Instead of the copper square, a paper clamp or suspender clip may be used to hold the galena.

About one or two inches from the crystal another nail or screw is driven into the baseboard. Before being driven tightly, one end of the cat-whisker wire which is about 3 inches long, is wound around this nail, as is also the end of a small piece of copper wire which runs to the phone binding-post. The loose end of the cat-whisker is curved, in an arc, so that it touches the crystal.

A wire from the ground binding-post runs to a water or steam pipe; but never a gas pipe, because it is an unreliable if not dangerous conductor. The pipe should be cleansed of all paint or corrosion at point of connection. Where there is no such pipe a copper plate about a foot square may be buried to a depth where the ground is always damp; or an iron pipe may be driven five or six feet into the ground. This plate or pipe is then connected to a wire which runs to the ground binding-post on the receiving set.

To operate this set the phone is placed to the ear, and the slider moved along the coil until transmitting signals can be heard. The cat-whisker is changed to different spots on the crystal until a contact is made that proves best. All connections should be tested now and then for security and sometimes a fresh lump of crystal and a new cat-whisker must be bought, but there is no other cost of up-keep.

Amplification of sound is possible with this set, but the purchase of the extra equipment required would mean an added expense approaching $200 for a two-stage amplifier with accompanying tubes and batteries, and a loud-speaker with horn. Good adjustment of the amplifier will yield as pure a tone as is yet obtainable with any set, but this amplification does not in any way increase the range of the set.

Experiments to date lead us to believe that satisfactory amplification is not to be expected by the average amateur when the volume of sound in the head-phone is weak. Many persons prefer head-phones to horns anyway, because they do not involve highly sensitive adjustment to obtain the same quality. How to make an amplifier and horn at a cost of $50 for materials is told in the description of the third, or advanced set.

The Intermediate Set

THE "intermediate set" is often called a "vacuum tube detector set" because a tube is used instead of a crystal. Ordinarily this set has a range of about 100 miles.

For the amateur, this is largely an assembled job. He buys the parts ready-made and connects them, or the set may be bought assembled.

The total cost, for the amateur who makes or assembles his set, is about $60.00, distributed as follows: Antenna, $1.50; lightning protector, $2.50; loose-coupler or other type of receiving transformer, $9.00; two variable condensers, $4.00 each; hard vacuum tube detector, $6.50; vacuum tube socket, $1.00; stopping condenser (.00025 microfarad) and grid leak (1 or 2 megohm), 50 cents; filament rheostat (6-ohm), $1.10; pair of 2,000-ohm phones, $8.00; an A or filament battery (6-volt, 80

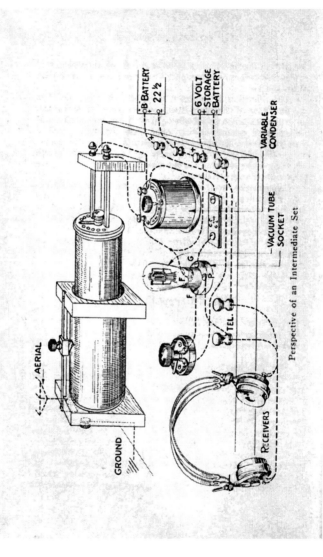

Perspective of an Intermediate Set

ampere-hour) storage, $15.00; a B or plate battery (22½-volt), $2.50. A loose-coupler may be manufactured by the amateur at a cost of $4.00 for materials. The only other thing to be made by him is the antenna.

Now, for a description of the parts and how they function. To begin with, let us understand that in the ABC, or elementary set, previously described, we had but one circuit for electrical energy; but that in the intermediate set we provide three circuits, namely: a primary (or first); a secondary (or second); and a detection amplifying circuit.

The first two circuits are for "selectivity"—in other words, obtaining a better rejection of interference, or, to express it still more simply, tuning out more of what we don't wish to hear than would be possible with but one circuit. The third circuit is for two purposes, detection as explained in the ABC set (the changing of the alternating current into direct current), and raising sound to a larger volume.

Taking up these three circuits one at a time we have:

Primary circuit—There are five instruments or parts that are linked in the primary circuit: (a) the antenna; (b) lightning protector; (c) slider tuning coil (called the primary inductance coil) and (d) a variable condenser which is connected with this coil and the ground. A variable condenser is an instrument to assist the slider in getting a finer adjustment of tuning. The slider tunes in, in steps, by sliding from one turn of wire on the coil to the next turn. But a step from one turn to the next is too large a jump for really fine adjustment, so the condenser is used to work in a closer adjustment between the turns. The fifth part of this circuit is (e) the ground connection.

Secondary circuit—There are two instruments or parts in the secondary circuit: (a) a secondary inductance coil; and (b) a variable condenser, just like the one in the first circuit. This secondary inductance coil is one that fits inside the primary inductance coil of the first circuit and is so arranged that the inside one can slide in and out of the outside one without touching it at any point. These two coils, when purchased, come assembled in one instrument called a "loose-coupler." This is how a loose-coupler works: Electric energies of different strengths, from different stations, come through the ether, down the antenna, to the primary coil. We wish to pass this current to the secondary coil, and a coupling is merely an arrangement of the primary and secondary coils for the passage of the current in a regulated way. When we say the coupling is "loose", we mean that, in the adjustment, the secondary coil has been slid far enough away from the primary so that only that particular energy which has been tuned in on the primary coil is strong enough to transfer through the intervening space to the secondary coil with any degree of strength— thus leaving behind most of the weak or rejected energies which we do not wish to receive. In this way we have what is called a loose inductive coupling—a passing of a selected energy from the primary to the secondary circuit without any wire connection between them.

Now that we have the coupling adjusted to receive the tuned-in wave from the primary circuit, we are ready to tune the secondary circuit in harmony (or resonance) with the primary—so that the selected energy may be passed along to the third circuit.

Detection-amplifying circuit—Here we are ready for detection (changing from an alternating to a direct current so that the phones will operate), and for amplifying the current so that we shall hear the sounds more plainly. In this, the third circuit, there are eight instruments or parts: (a) a hard vacuum tube; (b) a vacuum tube socket; (c) one B battery; (d) a pair of phones; (e) an A battery; (f) a filament current rheostat; (g) a grid condenser and with it (h) a grid leak.

First of importance in this last circuit is the vacuum tube. This serves as the detector (in place of the crystal in the ABC set) and it has a further purpose in that it is a medium for amplification.

This tube is called a 3-element vacuum tube because it

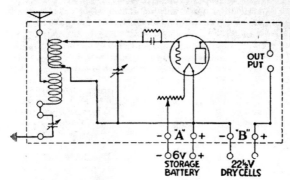

Schematic Showing Hook-up of Intermediate Set.

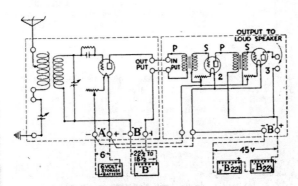

Schematic Showing Hook-up of Advanced Set.

has three elements in it: a filament, a grid, and a plate. The filament is a fine wire in the center of the tube; the grid, a wire mesh around the filament; the plate, small sheets of solid metal or a cylinder around the other two.

The purpose of the filament is to make the vacuum in the tube a conductor of current in this wise: From the filament, when heated, there come those minute particles of material called electrons (negative element of electricity) and ions (the positive element). These fill the space in the tube and make a conductor of it. The purpose of the grid is to regulate the amount and character of current passed through the vacuum. The purpose of the plate is to provide a means of carrying away the current from the tube.

In general there are two kinds of tubes, "soft" and "hard." The latter is more nearly a vacuum tube, that is, has more of the air pumped out of it. It is therefore called a high, or hard vacuum; the other a low, or soft, vacuum. Generally, soft tubes can be used only as detectors and not as amplifiers, and hard tubes only as amplifiers; but with the use of a grid condenser and a grid leak, which are hooked-up with the grid in the tube, a hard tube can be used in this set both as a detector and as an amplifier, at the same time rendering the volume of sound much greater than obtained in any other way.

The B battery is hooked into this circuit to increase the strength of the energy that is taken from the plate, so that it is passed along to the phones with the result that the volume of sound is estimated to be 25 times greater than from the best crystal detector. Some makes of hard tube require higher plate voltage. If 22½ volts are found to be insufficient, use 45 volts.

We use the A battery to heat the filament in the tube, it being one of the characteristics of the tube that it will not transmit energy until the filament is heated so as to free electrons and ions from it.

Now, we have to prevent this filament from burning out while we are making the little electrons and ions perform; so we have a filament rheostat (a resistance measurer) hooked-up with the filament, as a safety device to limit the amount of current going through it.

The second and third circuits are connected through the tube. The instruments and the circuits are hooked-up as shown in the sketch.

In order to receive with this set, the vacuum tube is lighted by rotating the rheostat lever; the secondary or inner-coil is set half-way inside the primary or outside coil. The variable condenser is turned at first to "minimum" as indicated on it. The secondary is varied in and out of the primary until the desired signal is heard, after which the variable condenser is adjusted until the maximum strength of that signal is obtained. A careful readjustment of the loose-coupler and of the variable condenser may produce increased selectivity and signal strength. The connection leading from the phones to the B battery should be moved from tap to tap as found on the battery, and the plate current thus increased or decreased until the maximum signal strength is obtained.

The cost of operating this set involves buying a new tube about every three months, ($6.50); charging the A battery every two weeks (75 cents); and replacing the B battery every three months ($2.50).

The Advanced Set

AN "advanced receiving set"—one still better than the intermediate—may be constructed within a total cost of $100 by using the intermediate set, previously described, as a base, making one change therein, and adding a two-stage amplifier and a home-made loud-speaker.

Vario-coupler—The change, an important one, consists of substituting for the loose-coupler a vario-coupler. Each of these instruments uses a pair of inductance coils, though the construction and operation of the pairs are different. In the vario-coupler, the primary coil is cylindrical and the secondary somewhat barrel-shaped, revolving on a fixed axis near one end of the cylinder.

Variations in the tuning of the inductance of the primary coil are obtainable by taps which are brought out from various turns in the primary coil to a multi-point switch. In tuning the primary, the variable condenser which is between the coil and the "ground" now plays a more important role in refined tuning, because it has to tune in at points between several turns of the primary coil as represented by the taps, instead of between just two turns as in the intermediate set.

The secondary of the vario-coupler has fewer turns of wire than the secondary of the loose-coupler, and in the former all turns are used in every adjustment. This means that we accomplish all tuning of the secondary by manipulating the condenser in the secondary circuit.

Since the secondary coil of the vario-coupler turns on its axis near one end of the primary instead of sliding in and out as in the case of the loose-coupler, a greater variation of coupling can be obtained with a vario-coupler —ranging from zero (when the secondary is set at right angles to the primary) on up to the maximum (when the two coils are parallel). A vario-coupler can be bought for about $6.

Amplifier—The parts of a two-stage amplifier and the cost thereof on the market are: Two inner-tube transformers, $5 each; 2 hard vacuum tubes, $6.50 each; 2 vacuum tube sockets, $1 each; 8 binding posts, 25 cents each; 2 six-ohm filament current rheostats, $1.10 each; 2 blocks of B battery (22½ volts), $2.50 each; suitable panel and box, rough materials for which could be bought for about $10. The A battery of the intermediate set can be used as filament current supply for amplifying tubes as well as for the detector tube.

Loud-speaker—A serviceable instrument can be made as follows: Procure at a cost of about $1 a sheet of zinc about 46x36 inches; cut and roll and solder to make a conical megaphone 36 inches long, 14 inches in diameter at the larger end and 1 inch in diameter at the smaller. With a piece of zinc about 3½x3 inches, make a tube 3 inches long and 1 inch in diameter to receive the small end

of the megaphone. Obtain two zinc caps from Mason
jars, and cut in the centers of them holes 1 inch in
diameter to receive the two ends of the little tube. Fit
the receivers of the head-phone in these caps and hold
them tightly in position by a spring or other contrivance.

The receivers used with this loud-speaker should be
modified as follows: Unscrew the caps and take out the
diaphragms, cut bond-linen paper washers the same size
as the diaphragms, with the inner diameter ½ inch less
than the outside diameter, the rim of the washer thus
being ¼ inch wide. Put these washers between the
diaphragms and the cups of the receivers and screw down
the caps. The washers are for the purpose of lifting the
diaphragms further from the pole pieces in the receivers
so that the diaphragms will vibrate more freely when
using the greater power.

Now we have a complete amplifier and loud-speaker
at a cost within about $50. While zinc is preferred to
other metals, a further improvement would result if
pasteboard, papier-mache or wood were used instead of
zinc in making the horn. There are also purchasable
devices which make possible the use of phonograph
horns.

Connecting and Operating—The amplifier and
loud-speaker are connected as shown in the wiring
diagram. To operate the amplifier, the filament current
rheostats are adjusted in the same manner as the rheostat of the intermediate set. The normal range of this
set is 150 miles; exceptional range 1,500 miles.

The cost of operating intermediate and advanced sets
is the same, except that, with the latter, two additional
vacuum tubes and the extra battery supply must be
maintained.

Note: There are two main types of so-called advanced sets—the vacuum-tube detecting and amplifying
set, as above described, and the "regenerative set" known
to many amateurs. The intermediate set can be given
a hook-up to make it a regenerative set and, with careful
handling, such a hook-up, with but one stage of amplifica-

tion, will give results nearly equal to a two-stage amplification with any other kind of a hook-up. But the regenerative hook-up as generally used by amateurs is not described here because it has been found to be objectionable on the ground that it is difficult to operate, and because oscillations in the detector tube make of the set a miniature transmitter which sends out waves at the same time it is receiving, and consequently cause interference with other nearby receiving sets.

A Simple Antenna

IN AN antenna or aerial that is to be used only for receiving, it is unnecessary to have more than one wire. For best results on the short waves the total length of the antenna (from the far end to the ground connection) should be 200 feet long, from 25 to 50 feet high, and should not run parallel to any electric light wires or under or through any branches of trees which might be blown against it. The wire used may be bare or insulated.

The further the receiving set is from the station, the more necessary it is to have a long, high antenna. While a 100-foot antenna, and even such makeshifts as bedsprings, give results near sending stations, it is advisable to provide a high class aerial composed of 200 feet of wire. This will make your set reach its maximum efficiency.

The flat-top (a) of the antenna as shown in the accompanying diagram and the antenna's lead-in (b) should be one continuous piece of wire; but, if in two separate pieces, then the connection at (c) should be soldered. (D) and (d) represent two high supports—mast, top of tree, or building—between which the flat-top (a) is stretched taut horizontally; (e) and (e) are insulators, which may be porcelain cleats or any other good strain variety, to which the flat-top (a) is fastened at (e) and (e). The insulators are in turn fastened to the supports (d) and (d) by means of pieces of wire or rope (f) and (f).

Diagram of a Simple Aerial.

The lead-in runs down to a lightning protector (g) or to a lightning switch. A protector is preferred to a switch; but when a switch is used the lead-in connects with the blade. (H) is a piece of pipe driven 5 or 6 feet into the ground and connected to the antenna through the protector or switch (g) by means of a piece of number four wire (i) to the receiving set, passing into the house through the window frame or casement by means of the porcelain tube (k). To keep the lead-in from touching the roof it may be necessary to pass it around or through an insulator on a support, as at (l).

The ground wire may be connected to a water or steam pipe, or to a piece of buried metal, or to both, but should not be attached to a gas pipe, which is unsatisfactory, if not dangerous.

Any lightning switch must be thrown to "ground position" for the period of any local thunder storm; and

it should also be at ground position when the set is not
in use. When a lightning protector is used in place of
a switch, of course there is no switch that need be thrown.
But with or without such a protector, no set should be
used during a period of near-by thunder and lightning.

Problems of the Amateur

FOLLOWING are answers to some of the questions
most commonly put to the technical staff of WWJ,
usually by beginners:

Ques.—Would an aerial consisting of 100 feet of wire
made up in four strands 25 feet long be as good as a single wire 100 feet in length for receiving the broadcasts?

Ans.—The single 100-foot wire is much better than
the four-wire, 25-foot aerial.

Ques.—How far can I receive with a crystal detector
receiving set?

Ans.—The distance at which you can receive with any
type of detector depends on the power of the transmitting station whose signals you desire to hear. There is a
great difference, however, in the sensitiveness of various
detectors, the crystal being much less efficient than the
vacuum tube. Judging by correspondence received at
WWJ the crystal detector can be depended on to receive
Detroit News concerts at a distance of from 25 to 50
miles. Many letters indicate our signals have been heard
as far as 250 miles, but this is not common. One amateur
reports hearing WWJ 445 miles away with a home made
crystal detector set.

Ques.—Is it necessary to have a government license
to operate a receiving set?

Ans.—No. A government license is only necessary
when one operates a sending station in the United States,
but laws recently enacted in Canada specify licenses for
both sending and receiving stations.

Ques.—Can I use insulated wire for an aerial?

Ans.—Insulated wire is just as satisfactory as bare
wire.

The Detroit Symphony Orchestra, Whose Concerts Are Broadcast by WWJ

Ques.—How many stages of amplification are necessary to operate a loud speaker?

Ans.—In general at least two stages of amplification will be needed.

Ques.—Can a loud speaker be attached to a crystal detector receiving set?

Ans.—Generally the results are not satisfactory owing to the fact that the crystal detector does not pass enough current.

Ques.—Can I amplify the signals from a crystal detector?

Ans.—The signals can be amplified, but generally the results are not entirely satisfactory owing to the fact that a crystal detector set does not receive signals of a sufficient strength unless it is within a very few miles of a powerful transmitting station.

Ques.—Why am I not able to receive Chicago and Pittsburgh? I use a crystal detector.

Ans.—In general, the crystal detector is not sensitive enough to receive from such distant points.

Ques.—What kind of condenser is best for keeping the alternating house current out of my receiving set when using the light wires for my antenna?

Ans.—A fixed condenser with mica insulation is preferable to one with paper insulation. About 20 square inches of tin foil should be used to make the condenser.

Ques.—Is a lightning switch needed for an inside aerial?

Ans.—The underwriters do not require a lightning switch for an indoor aerial.

Ques.—May an amateur use his transmitting set during the time that a concert is being broadcast?

Ans.—The amateur has as much right to transmit as the broadcasting station, providing he does not cause extreme interference with those who are listening to the broadcast. In general, a C. W. set working on the amateur wave length of 200 meters will not interfere. The spark transmitter probably will interfere, even though tuned very sharply to 200 meters.

Ques.—Can I attach my aerial to the telephone or electric light poles, and does it matter if the aerial wires cross the house lighting wires?

Ans.—Permission should be obtained from the owners before aerials are fastened to poles. The Detroit Edison Co. does not permit anyone to use its poles. Aerial wires must never run across or parallel to any power or lighting wires.

Ques.—Is there any danger attached to radio receiving?

Ans.—None whatever excepting danger from lightning, obviated by lightning arresters or switches, and from lack of caution in erecting antenna in the neighborhood of light or power lines. Receiving sets themselves are harmless.

Ques.—What are the means of preventing damage by lightning striking an aerial?

Ans.—The best device is a lightning protector, purchasable at any radio supply house, and accompanied by directions for installing. Next best is a so-called lightning or ground switch. However, it is also possible to avoid danger during electrical storms by detaching aerial and ground wires from the receiving set, fastening them together so as to form an electrical connection, insulating with friction tape and throwing them out the window. Then, if you have a fixed ground, lightning, if it strikes the aerial, will pass to the earth.

Ques.—Is it possible to use loud speakers and not have objectionable overtones, or horn noises such as characterized old-fashioned phonographs?

Ans.—Yes. Freedom from such noises depends wholly upon the equipment. A high class set, properly installed and operated, will yield a pure tone if the loud speaking equipment is also high class.

Ques.—Which is clearest and purest in tone, within proper range, crystal or vacuum tube detector?

Ans.—Probably most people will get clearest and purest tones from crystal sets. The vacuum tube sets can be tuned down to the same purity, but few are willing to sacrifice strength for quality.

Ques.—What ohmage in head phones gives best results?

Ans.—Any standard make phone of 2000 or more ohms will give good results under proper conditions. If you have a crystal detector set, get such phones and then try out crystals until you get one which gives best results. The mere fact that a set is of 3000 ohms resistance does not necessarily mean that it is better than a 2000 ohm set. Any standard make of 2000 ohms or more should give good results with vacuum tube sets properly constructed and operated. Some unscrupulous manufacturers have wound pole pieces with high resistance wire, thereby giving high ohmage to phones, but the result is a decidedly inferior set.

Ques.—What should be the relative size of ground and lead-in wires?

Ans.—Ground wires should always be larger than aerial and lead-in. The insurance underwriters specify No. 4 ground wires. Lead-in wires need not be heavy; No. 14 is commonly used.

Ques.—Is there any loss in receiving if aerial and lead-in are made of various sizes of wire, pieced together?

Ans.—It is better to have only the one piece of wire; but properly connected at all junctions (preferably with solder) your patchwork antenna will give good results.

Ques.—Can I use two receiving sets on one aerial and get good results?

Ans.—Two receiving sets cannot be used on one aerial with any degree of satisfaction since tuning one set puts the other out of tune; also two sets on one aerial reduce signal strength. By chance, two sets may give surprisingly good results on a single antenna if near a powerful sending station, but such results are to be classed as freakish.

The Michigan Glee Club, Singing for the First College Reunion by Radio

Government Regulations

UNDER the Act of Congress of August 13, 1912, amateurs are forbidden to transmit interstate messages by radio without a license issued by the Department of Commerce. When the effect of such transmission does not extend beyond the jurisdiction of the state in question the transmission without license is permissible.

Any transmitting station which interferes with the receipt of messages from stations in other states must have a license, even though its own messages are kept within the state in which it is located. Of course no license is required in this country for receiving sets.

Some of the regulations in force in 1922 affecting amateurs and also commercial broadcasting stations may be summarized thus:

At all stations, if the transmitter is of such a character that energy can be radiated in two or more wave lengths, the energy in no one of the lesser waves shall exceed 10 per cent of that in the greatest.

All stations are required to give absolute priority to signals and radiograms relating to ships in distress.

All stations shall use the minimum amount of power necessary to carry on reliable communication, except in the case of ships in distress.

No person shall divulge the contents of messages coming to his knowledge.

Misdemeanors in the radio field are punishable by fines ranging from $25 to $5,000, and in many cases involve the revocation of the offender's license. Some of these offenses are:

Wilfully interfering with any other radio communication.

Transmitting false signals or fraudulent messages of any kind.

Operating without a license, which is punishable by a fine of $500 and confiscation of equipment.

Those living in Detroit who wish to transmit should make application to the United States Radio Inspector,

405 Postoffice Building, Detroit, Mich. The way to communicate with any other district headquarters is to address the letter to the United States Radio Inspector, naming the district and the city where his office is.

America is divided into nine districts, the geographical divisions of which follow, the city named in each case being the headquarters for that district:

1. Boston, Mass.: Maine, New Hampshire, Vermont, Massachusetts, Rhode Island, Connecticut.

2. New York, N. Y.: New York (county of New York, Staten Island, Long Island, and counties on the Hudson River to and including Schenectady, Albany and Rensselaer) and New Jersey (counties of Bergen, Passaic, Essex, Union, Middlesex, Monmouth, Hudson and Ocean).

3 and 4. Baltimore, Md.: New Jersey (all counties not included in second district), Pennsylvania (counties south of the Blue Mountains, and Franklin County), Delaware, Maryland, Virginia, District of Columbia, North Carolina, South Carolina, Florida, Porto Rico.

5. New Orleans, La.: Alabama, Mississippi, Louisiana, Texas, Tennessee, Arkansas, Oklahoma, New Mexico.

6. San Francisco, Calif.: California, Hawaii, Nevada, Utah, Arizona.

7. Seattle, Wash.: Oregon, Washington, Alaska, Idaho, Montana, Wyoming.

8. Detroit, Mich.: Michigan (Lower Peninsula), New York (all counties, excepting counties on the Hudson River up to and including Rensselaer County), Pennsylvania (counties not in the 3rd and 4th districts), and all of West Virginia and Ohio.

9. Chicago, Ill.: Indiana, Illinois, Wisconsin, Michigan (Upper Peninsula), Minnesota, Kentucky, Missouri, Kansas, Colorado, Iowa, Nebraska, South Dakota, North Dakota.

Directory of Broadcasting Stations

WWJ is not a person. WWJ is The Detroit News radiophone station. WWJ is not the initials of any name. It is a symbol. It was issued to The Detroit News by the Government in connection with the Federal licensing of this broadcasting plant. When the thousands of members of the Detroit News radio family hear a voice saying, "This is WWJ, The Detroit News," they hear a voice that personifies this station and this radiophone service—but it isn't always the same voice. It may be a different voice for the various schedules of the day, but always the voice speaks for the whole radiophone service of The Detroit News.

All private broadcasting call signals in America begin with either W or K. All U. S. Navy station calls begin with N. This alphabetical allotment to America was made by the International Radiotelegraphic Convention.

Following is an alphabetical list of the broadcasting stations licensed by the Government up to May 15, 1922. Revised lists are published in the "Radio Service Bulletin," issued monthly by the Government and procurable from the Superintendent of Documents, Government Printing Office, Washington, D. C.

Owner of Station.	Location of Station.	Wave Lengths.	Call Signal.
Alabama Power Co	Birmingham, Ala.	360	WSY
Alamo Radio Electric Co	San Antonio, Tex.	360	WCAR
Aldrich Marble & Granite Co., C. F.	Colorado Springs, Col.	485	KHD
Allen, Preston D	Oakland, Calif.	360	KZM
Altadena Radio Laboratory	Altadena, Calif.	360	KGO
American Radio & Research Corp.	Medford Hillside, Mass	360	WGI
American Tel. & Tel. Co.	New York City	360	WBAY
Anthony, Earl C	Los Angeles, Calif.	360	KFI
Arrow Radio Laboratories	Anderson, Ind.	360	WMA
Athens Radio Co.	Athens, Ga.	360	WAAV
Atlanta Journal	Atlanta, Ga.	360, 485	WSB
Atlantic-Pacific Radio Supplies Co.	Oakland, Calif.	360	KZY
Auburn Electrical Co	Auburn, Me.	360	WMB

Bakersfield Californian	Bakersfield, Calif.	360	KYI
Bamberger & Co., L.	Newark, N. J.	360	WOR
Beacon Light Co.	Los Angeles, Calif.	360	KNR
Benwood Co.	St. Louis, Mo.	360	WEB
Bible Institute of Los Angeles	Los Angeles, Calif.	360	KJS
Blue Diamond Electric Co.	Hood River, Ore.	360	KQP
Bradley Poly. Institute	Peoria, Ill.	360	WBAE
Braun Corporation	Los Angeles, Calif.	360	KXS
Buckeye Radio Service Co.	Akron, O.	360	WOE
Bullock's	Los Angeles, Calif.	360	KNN
Bush, James L.	Tuscola, Ill.	360	WDZ
Carlson & Simpson	San Diego, Calif.	360	KDYO
Central Radio Co.	Kansas City, Mo.	360	WPE
Central Radio Service	Decatur, Ill.	360	WCAP
Church of the Covenant	Washington, D. C.	360	WDM
Chicago, City of	Chicago, Ill.	360	WBU
Cino Radio Mfg. Co.	Cincinnati, O.	360, 485	WIZ
City Dye Works & Laundry Co.	Los Angeles, Calif.	360	KUS
Clark University	Worcester, Mass.	360, 485	WCN
Coast Radio Co.	Elmont, Calif.	360	KUY
Columbia Radio Co.	Youngstown, O.	360	WMC
Commonwealth Electric Co.	St. Paul, Minn.	360	WAAH
Continental Elec. Supply Co.	Washington, D. C.	360	WIL
Cooper, Irving S.	Los Angeles, Calif.	360	KZI
Cosradio Co.	Wichita, Kans.	360 485	WEY
Cox, Warren R.	Cleveland, Ohio.	360	WHK
Crosley Mfg. Co.	Cincinnati, O.	360, 485	WLW
Daily News Printing Co.	Canton, O.	360	WWB
Daily States Pub. Co.	New Orleans, La.	360	WCAG
Dallas, City of	Dallas, Tex.	360, 485	WRR
Daniel, Alfred P.	Houston, Tex.	360	WCAK
Dayton Co.	Minneapolis, Minn.	360	WBAP
DeForest Radio Co.	New York, N. Y.	360	WJX
Deseret News	Salt Lake City, Utah.	360	KZN
DETROIT NEWS	DETROIT, MICH.	360, 485	WWJ
Detroit Police Department	Detroit, Mich.	360	KOP
Diamond State Fibre Co.	Bridgeport, Pa.	360, 485	WBAG
Doerr-Mitchell Elec. Co.	Spokane, Wash.	360	KFZ
Doron Brothers Elec. Co.	Hamilton, O.	360	WRK
Doubleday-Hill Elec. Co.	Pittsburgh, Pa.	360	KQV
Doubleday-Hill Elec. Co.	Washington, D. C.	360	WMU
Duck Co., William B.	Toledo, O.	360, 485	WHU
Dunn & Co., J. J.	Pasadena, Calif.	360	KLB
Eastern Radio Institute	Boston, Mass.	360	WAAJ
Electric Equipment Co.	Erie, Pa.	360	WJT
Electric Lighting & Supply Co.	Hollywood, Calif.	360	KGC
Electric Lighting Supply Co.	Los Angeles, Calif.	360	KNX
Electric Power & Appliance Co.	Yakima, Wash.	360	KQT
Electric Supply Co.	Clearfield, Pa.	360	WPI
Elliott Electric Co.	Shreveport, La.	360	WAAG
Emporium, The	San Francisco, Calif.	360	KSL
Erie Radio Co.	Erie, Pa.	360	WSX
Erner & Hopkins Co., The	Columbus, O.	360	WBAV
Examiner Printing Co.	San Francisco, Calif.	360	KUO
Fair, The	Chicago, Ill.	360	WGU

Federal Inst. of Radio Telegraphy..Camden, N. J........ 360		WRP
Federal Telephone & Telegraph Co..Buffalo, N. Y....... 360, 485		WGR
Fergus Electric Co................Zanesville, O. 360		WPL
Findley Electric Co...............Minneapolis, Minn... 300		WCE
First Presbyterian Church........Seattle, Wash. 360		KTW
Ford Motor Co....................Dearborn, Mich. 360		WWI
Fort Worth Record................Fort Worth, Tex..... 360		WPA
Foster-Bradbury Radio Store.......Yakima, Wash. 360		KFV
Free Press, The...................Detroit, Mich. 360, 485		WCX
General Electric Co...............Schenectady, N. Y... 360		WGY
Georgia Radio Co..................Atlanta, Ga. 360		WAAS
Georgia Railway & Power Co. (Atlanta Constitution) ....Atlanta, Ga. 360, 485		WGM
Gilbert Co., A. C.................New Haven, Conn.... 360		WCJ
Gimbel Brothers ....Philadelphia, Pa. 360		WIP
Gimbel Brothers ....Milwaukee, Wis. 360		WAAK
Gould, C. O.......................Stockton, Calif. 360		KJQ
Great Western Radio Corp........Redwood City, Calif.. 360		KDYN
Groves-Thorton Hardware Co.......Huntington, W. Va.. 360		WAAR
Hale, O. A. & Co.................San Jose, Cal........ 360		KSC
Hale Bros., Inc...................San Francisco, Calif. 360		KPO
Halleck & Watson Radio Service...Portland, Ore. 360		KGG
Hamilton Mfg. Co.................Indianapolis, Ind.... 360		WLK
Harmon, Myron (Y. M. C. A.).....South Bend, Ind.... 360		WBAQ
Hatfield Electric Co..............Indianapolis, Ind.... 360		WOH
Hawley, Willard P. Jr............Portland, Ore. 360		KYG
Herald Publishing Co.............Modesto, Calif. 360		KXD
Herrold, Charles D................San Jose, Calif. 360		KQW
Hobrecht, J. C...................Sacramento, Calif. ... 360		KVQ
Hollister-Miller Motor Co.........Emporia, Kans. 360		WAAZ
Holzwasser Inc. ....San Diego, Calif..... 360		KON
Howe, Richard H.................Granville, O. 360		WJD
Howlett, Thomas F. J.............Philadelphia, Pa. ... 360		WGL
Hunter, L. M. & G. L. Carrington..Little Rock, Ark..... 360		WSV
Hurlburt Still Electrical Co........Houston, Tex. 360, 485		WEV
Interstate Electric Co.............New Orleans, La..... 360		WGV
Iowa Radio Corporation............Des Moines, Ia...... 360		WHX
Iowa State College................Ames, Iowa 360, 485		WOI
James Milliken University.........Decatur, Ill. 360		WBAO
John Fink Jewelry Co.............Fort Smith, Ark..... 360		WCAC
J. & M. Electric Co...............Utica, N. Y......... 360		WSL
K. & L. Electric Co...............McKeesport, Pa. 360		WIK
Kansas State Agri. College........Manhattan, Kans. ... 485		WTG
Karlowa Radio Co................Rock Island, Ill..... 360, 485		WOC
Kaufmann & Baer Co.............Pittsburgh, Pa. 360		WCAE
Kennedy Co., Colin B............Los Altos, Calif...... 360		KLP
Kierulff & Co., C. R.............Los Angeles, Calif.... 360		KHJ
Kluge, Arno A...................Los Angeles, Calif.... 000		KQL
Kraft, Vincent I.................Seattle, Wash. 360, 485		KJR
Lindsay-Weatherill & Co..........Reedley, Calif. 360		KMC
Lorden, Edwin L.................San Francisco, Calif.. 360		KGB
Los Angeles Examiner.............Los Angeles, Calif.... 360		KWH
Love Electric Co.................Tacoma, Wash. 360		KMO
Loyola University ....New Orleans, La...... 360		WWL
Marietta College ....Marietta, O. 360		WBAW

Marshall-Gerkin Co.	Toledo, O.	360, 485	WBAJ
Maxwell Electric Co.	Berkeley, Calif.	360	KRE
May, (Inc.) D. W.	Newark, N. J.	360	WBS
McBride, George M.	Bay City, Mich.	360	WTP
McCarthy Bros. & Ford	Buffalo, N. Y.	360	WWT
Metropolitan Utilities Dist.	Omaha, Neb.	360, 485	WOU
Meyberg Co., Leo J.	Los Angeles, Calif.	360, 485	KYJ
Meyberg Co., Leo J.	San Francisco, Calif.	360, 485	KDN
Middleton, Fred M.	Moorestown, N. J.	360	WBAF
Midland Refining Co.	El Dorado, Kans.	485	WAH
Midland Refining Co.	Tulsa, Okla.	485	WEh
Minnesota Tribune Co. & Anderson-Beamish Co.	Minneapolis, Minn.	360	WAAL
Missouri State Marketing Bureau	Jefferson City, Mo.	485	WOS
Modesto Evening News	Modesto, Calif.	360	KOQ
Montgomery Light & Power Co.	Montgomery, Ala.	360, 485	WGH
Mullins Electric Co., Wm. A.	Tacoma, Wash.	360	KGB
Mulrony, Marion A.	Honolulu, Hawaii.	360	KGU
Nebraska Wesleyan University	Lincoln, Neb.	360, 485	WCAJ
Nelson Co., I. R.	Newark, N. J.	360	WAAM
Newburg News Ptg. & Pub. Co.	Newburg, N. Y.	360	WCAB
New England Motor Sales Co.	Greenwich, Conn.	360	WAAQ
New Mexico College	State College, N. Mex	360, 485	KOB
Newspaper Printing Co.	Pittsburgh, Pa.	360	WPB
Noggle Electric Works	Monterey, Calif.	360	KLN
North Coasts Products Co.	Aberdeen, Wash.	360	KNT
Northern Radio & Electric Co.	Seattle, Wash.	360	KFC
Northwestern Radio Co.	Portland, Ode.	360	KGN
Nushawg Poultry Farm	New Lebanon, O.	360	WPG
Oklahoma Radio Shop	Oklahoma City, Okla.	360, 485	WKY
Omaha Grain Exchange	Omaha, Neb.	360	WAAW
Oregon Inst. of Technology	Portland, Ore.	485	KDYQ
Oregonian Publishing Co.	Portland, Ore.	360	KGW
Palladium Printing Co.	Richmond, Ind.	360	WOZ
Palmer School of Chiropractic	Davenport, Iowa	360, 485	WOC
Paris Radio Electric Co.	Paris, Tex.	360	WTK
Pasadena Star-News	Pasadena, Calif.	360	KDYR
Penna. State Police	Harrisburgh, Pa.	360	WBAK
Philadelphia Radiophone Co.	Philadelphia, Pa.	360	WCAU
Pine Bluff Co.	Pine Bluff, Ark.	360	WOK
Potter, Andrew J.	Syracuse, N. Y.	360	WBAB
Pomona Fixture & Wiring Co.	Pomona, Calif.	360	KGF
Portable Wireless Telephone Co.	Stockton, Calif.	360	KWG
Post Dispatch	St. Louis, Mo.	360	KSD
Precision Equipment Co.	Cincinnati, O.	360, 485	WMH
Precision Shop, The	Gridley, Calif.	360	KFU
Prest & Dean Radio Research Lab.	Long Beach, Calif.	360	KSS
Public Market and Dept. Stores.	Seattle, Wash.	360	KZC
Purdue University	West Lafayette, Ind.	360	WBAA
Radio Construction & Electric Co.	Washington, D. C.	360	WDW
Radio Corporation of America	Roselle Park, N. J.	360	WDY
Radio Service Corp.	Pittsburgh, Pa.	360	WAAX
Radio Service Co.	Charleston, W. Va.	360	WAAO
Radio Shop, The	Sunnyvale, Calif.	360	KJJ
Radio Supply Co.	Los Angeles, Calif.	360	KNV

Radio Telephone Shop, The	San Francisco, Calif.	360	KYY
Register & Tribune, The	Des Moines, Ia.	360	WGF
Renn sen, I. B.	New Orleans, La.	360	WBMA
Rep. lican Pub. Co.	Hamilton, O.	360	WBAU
Reynolds Radio Co.	Denver, Colo.	360, 485	KLZ
Ridgewood, Times & Co.	Ridgewood, N. Y.	360	WHN
Riechman-Crosby Co.	Memphis, Tenn.	360, 485	WKN
Rike-Kumler Co.	Dayton, O.	360, 485	WFO
Rochester Times-Union	Rochester, N. Y.	360, 485	WHQ
Roswell Public Service Co.	Roswell, N. Mex.	360, 485	KNJ
St. Joseph's College	Philadelphia, Pa.	360	WPJ
St. Lawrence University	Canton, N. Y.	485	WCAD
St. Louis Chamber of Commerce	St. Louis, Mo.	360	WAAE
St. Louis University	St. Louis, Mo.	485	WEW
St. Martin's College (Rev. S. Ruth)	Lacey, Wash.	360	KGY
St. Olaf College	Northfield, Minn	360	WCAL
Sanders & Stayman Co.	Baltimore, Md.	360	WCAO
San Joaquin Light & Power Co 'p.	Fresno, Calif.	360	KMJ
Savoy Theater	San Diego, Calif.	360	KDYM
Seeley, Stuart W.	East Lansing, Mich.	485	WHW
Service Radio Equipment Co.	Toledo, O.	300	WJK
Ship Owners Radio Service	New York, N. Y.	360	WDT
Ship Owners Radio Service	Norfolk, Va.	360	WSN
Shotton Radio Co.	Albany, N. Y.	360	WNJ
Smith, T. W.	Eureka, Calif.	360	KNI
Southeastern Radio Tel. Co.	Jacksonville, Fla.	360	WCAN
Southern Electrical Co.	San Diego, Calif.	360	KDPT
Southern Radio Corp.	Charlotte, N. C.	360	WBT
South Dakota School of Mines	Rapid City, S. D.	485	WCAT
Spokane Chronicle	Spokane, Wash.	360	KOE
Standard Radio Co.	Los Angeles, Calif.	360	KJC
Stenger, John H., Jr.	Wilkes-Barre, Pa.	300	WBAX
Sterling El. Co. & Journal Ptg. Co.	Minneapolis, Minn.	360	WBAD
Stix-Baer-Fuller	St. Louis, Mo.	360	WCK
Strawbridge & Clothier	Philadelphia, Pa.	360	WFI
Stubbs Electric Co.	Portland, Ore.	360	KQY
T. & H. Radio Co.	Anthony, Kans.	360	WBL
Tarrytown Radio Research Lab.	Tarrytown, N. Y.	360	WRW
Taylor, Otto W.	Wichita, Kans.	360	WAAP
Thearle Music Co.	San Diego, Calif.	360	KYF
Times-Dispatch Pub. Co.	Richmond, Va.	360	WBAZ
Times-Picayune Publishing Co.	New Orleans, La.	360	WAAB
Tribune Pub. Co.	Oakland, Calif.	360	KLX
Tri-State Radio Mfg. & Sup. Co.	Defiance, O.	300	WCAQ
Tulane University	New Orleans, La.	360	WAAC
Union College.	Schenectady, N. Y.	360	WRL
Union Stock Yards & Transit Co.	Chicago, Ill.	360, 485	WAAF
United Equipment Co.	Memphis, Tenn.	360	WPO
University of California	Berkeley, Calif.	360	KQI
University of Illinois	Urbana, Ill.	360	WRM
University of Minnesota	Minneapolis, Minn.	360, 485	WLB
University of Missouri	Columbia, Mo.	360	WAAN
University of Nevada	Reno, Nev.	360	KOJ
University of Texas	Austin, Tex.	360, 485	WCM
University of Wisconsin	Madison, Wis.	360, 485	WHA

Villanova College .... Villanova, Pa. 360   WAM
Wanamaker, John .... Philadelphia, Pa. ... 360   WOO
Wanamaker, John .... New York, N. Y...... 360   WWZ
Warner Brothers .... Oakland, Calif. 360   KLS
Wasmer, Louis .... Seattle, Wash. 360   KHQ
Wenatchee Battery & Motor Co..... Wenatchee, Wash.... 360   KZV
Western Radio Co.................. Kansas City, Mo.... 360, 485   WOQ
Western Radio Electric Co......... Los Angeles, Calif... 360   KOG
Westinghouse Electric Co.......... East Pittsburgh, Pa. 360   KDKA
Westinghouse Electric Co......... Chicago, Ill. .... 360, 485   KYW
Westinghouse Electric Co.......... Newark, N. J........ 360   WJZ
Westinghouse Electric Co.......... Springfield, Mass..... 360   WBZ
West Virginia University.......... Morgantown, W. Va. 360   WHD
White & Boyer Co................. Washington, D. C.... 360   WJH
William, Thomas J................. Washington, D. C.... 360   WPM
Wm. Hood Dunwoody Institute..... Minneapolis, Minn.... 360   WCAS
Wireless Phone Corp.............. Paterson, N. J....... 360   WBAN
Wireless Telephone Co............ Jersey City, N. J.... 360   WNO
Wortham-Carter Pub. Co. (The Star
   Telegram) .... Fort Worth, Tex..... 360   WBAP
Yahrling-Rayner Piano Co......... Youngstown, O. 360   WAAY
Yelser, John O. Jr................ Omaha, Neb. 360   WDV
Y. M. C. A....................... Denver, Colo. 485   KOA
Zamoiski Co., Joseph M........... Baltimore, Md. 360   WKC

Glossary of Radio Terms

A. C.—Abbreviation for alternating current.

Acoustic waves—Commonly called "sound waves." Waves due to expansion of a solid, liquid or gas after a temporary compression. Propagation of sound through water depends on this class of wave. In air, their velocity is 1090-1132 feet per second at 75 degrees Fahrenheit.

Aerial—That part of an antenna system composed of one or several wires suspended above ground and insulated from all surrounding objects. Used to facilitate generation of ether waves for radio transmission or absorb same for reception.

Aerial insulation—Insulation between aerial and its supports. Does not refer to any covering of the aerial wires, which are generally bare.

Aerial switch—A switch used to change over from transmission to reception, also called "change-over switch."

Aerial wire—Wire forming the aerial. Carried in stock by all first class jobbers and dealers.

Aerial tuning condenser—Variable condenser in antenna circuit. Used to vary oscillation constant of antenna system.

Alternating current—Current which flows for a short period of time in one direction and then reverses, flowing in the opposite direction for an equal period of time.

Ammeter—Instrument for measuring current in amperes. It is connected in series with the circuit. Exists in a variety of forms, the most common of which depends upon the fact that the force a magnet exerts depends upon the number of ampere-turns. Therefore the greater the number of amperes sent through its coils the greater will be its attraction of a balanced armature.

Amp.—See Ampere.

Air condenser—One having air as the dielectric.

Ampere—Unit of current.

Ampere hour—That current which flows in one hour through a circuit, carrying a steady current of one ampere. Is equal to 3600 coulombs. Ampere-minute and ampere-second are the same, but for the altered time value.

Amplifier—A device used to magnify small radio or audio frequency currents. Several of these devices may be used in series, making a two or multi-stage amplifier.

Antenna—Same as aerial.

Antenna circuit—Consists of aerial and earth connection, including all coils and condensers which may be between these, forming a direct path from aerial to earth.

Arrester, lightning—(a) A lightning switch which needs to be thrown in connecting the aerial with the ground wire. (b) An automatic protective device put in the circuit to carry away and discharge all charges of lightning.

Batteries—"A" Batteries are 6-volt or 12-volt batteries, used as a source of supply for vacuum tube filaments, in transmitting and receiving. "B" Batteries are standard 22 to 27-volt storage or dry cell batteries. They are used as a source of supply for the plate circuit.

Buzzer—Similar to an electric bell with hammer and gong removed. Used to adjust receiving detectors by exciting the local detector circuit. Also used for tone or buzzer modulated transmission.

Cage aerial—One consisting of a number of component wires held in position by hoop spreaders. Used during the war on naval vessels, because of the facility with which they could be replaced when shot away in battle.

Capacity—Power of containing. A condenser has unit capacity (farad) when a charge of one coulomb creates a difference of potential of one volt between its terminals. The farad, being too large for practical purposes, the microfarad (one millionth of a farad) is used, or a micro micro farad (one millionth part of a micro farad).

Carrying capacity—Amount of current a conductor can safely carry without becoming unduly heated.

Cascade—Term applied to a number of pieces of apparatus connected up in series.

Choke coils—Coils wound to have great self-inductance. Usually wound over an iron core, composed of a bundle of wires, or laminated sheets, insulated from each other to prevent eddy currents. Their function is to check by reactance the amount of current flowing in the circuit. The choking effect is called impedance.

Chopper—Another name for "tone wheel." A mechanical interrupter, usually taking the form of a wheel, interrupting radio-frequency oscillations to make audio-frequency oscillations, that is, oscillations audible to the human ear.

Circuit—The continuous path in which a current of electricity may flow.

Close Coupling—Exists where primary and secondary of oscillation or receiving transformer are very close together when inductively coupled; or if directly coupled when a large proportion of the turns are common. Causes great mutual inductance.

Condenser—Two or more sheets of metal separated by an insulator called the dielectric which form a collector of electrical potential energy.

Continuous current—Direct current, D. C., one flowing constantly and regularly in one direction. In practice is produced by an arc discharge in place of spark; also by an oscillating vacuum tube or high frequency alternator.

Counterpoise—An artificial "earth" with regard to the aerial. Also used where good ground connection is not available.

Critical point—That point on the characteristic curve of a crystal or vacuum tube detector at which rectification is most complete.

Crystals—Bornite, Carborundum, Copper Pyrites, Galena, Tellurium, Iron Pyrites, Cerusite, Perikon, Silicon, Sylvanite and Zincite. Used for rectification or detection of small radio frequency current.

Crystal detector—One depending upon the fact that certain combinations of metallic crystals or of crystals and metals permit a current to pass more readily in one direction than the other thus having a rectifying effect upon a train of oscillations, to act upon a sensitive telephone receiver.

D. C.—Abbreviation for direct current.

Diaphragm—Thin disc in a telephone receiver unit which sets up the audible sound waves from vibrations caused by the periodic attractions of the telephone magnets.

Direct coupling—A coupling in which the inductance coils of both primary and secondary circuits are metallically connected. One in which all or part of turns are common to both circuits.

Direct current—Current flowing continuously in one direction. Continuous current.

Double pole switch—One which simultaneously makes or breaks two wires of a circuit.

Down lead—Lead in. Wire connecting elevated portion of aerial to the receiver instruments.

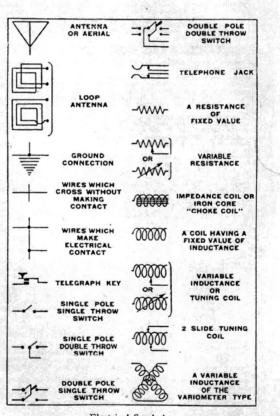

ANTENNA OR AERIAL	DOUBLE POLE DOUBLE THROW SWITCH
	TELEPHONE JACK
LOOP ANTENNA	A RESISTANCE OF FIXED VALUE
GROUND CONNECTION	VARIABLE RESISTANCE
WIRES WHICH CROSS WITHOUT MAKING CONTACT	IMPEDANCE COIL OR IRON CORE "CHOKE COIL"
WIRES WHICH MAKE ELECTRICAL CONTACT	A COIL HAVING A FIXED VALUE OF INDUCTANCE
TELEGRAPH KEY	VARIABLE INDUCTANCE OR TUNING COIL
SINGLE POLE SINGLE THROW SWITCH	2 SLIDE TUNING COIL
SINGLE POLE DOUBLE THROW SWITCH	A VARIABLE INDUCTANCE OF THE VARIOMETER TYPE
DOUBLE POLE SINGLE THROW SWITCH	

Electrical Symbols.

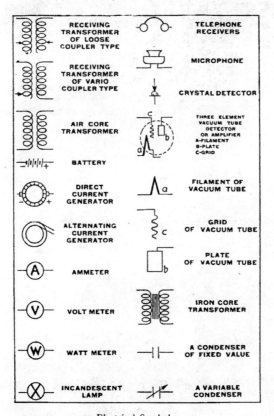

Electrical Symbols.

Electricity—From Greek word "Elektron," meaning amber. One of the earliest known methods of producing electric charges was by rubbing amber with silk. The word was first used by Dr. Gilbert of Colchester in the year 1600.

Electron—Ultimate or final particle of negative electricity. An atom plus an electron is a negative ion. An atom minus an electron is a positive ion.

Electron flow—The electron emission from a heated filament in the vacuum tube.

E. M. F.—Electromotive force. Unit is volt, which is that electric potential which causes one ampere to flow through a circuit which has a resistance of one ohm.

Fading—Phenomena causing distant radio signals to vary in intensity. Caused by atmospheric conditions.

Farad—See Capacity.

Galena—PbS. A natural crystal, sulphite of lead. Also called lead glance. Has a blue-gray color similar to freshly cut lead. When heated in air, becomes lead sulphate (PbSo). The cubical crystal is a non-potential rectifier. Most sensitive popular crystal for use in radio reception.

Grid—The frame of wire or perforated metal plate placed between and insulated from the plate and filament of a vacuum tube. Also refers to leaden framework holding paste of storage battery plates.

Grid-Leak—A very high resistance used in shunt connection with the grid condenser in the grid lead of a vacuum tube to allow negative ions collected on the grid to leak off to the filament. Hard amplifier tubes as detectors with the condenser require such, or they will choke, giving no signals, and a put-put-put in the phones.

Ground circuit—One employing earth as one "wire." The earth is generally used for the negative or return side of a circuit.

Ground wires—Wires giving connection to the earth.

H. F. Choke—High frequency choke coil. Similar to choke coil, except with air core.

Henry—Unit of inductance. That inductance in a circuit when current is changing at rate of one ampere per second and producing a difference of potential of one volt across the inductance.

Horse power—Power required to perform 550 foot-pounds of work per second. 746 watts equal one horse-power.

Impedance coil—A coil of wire wound over a soft-iron core. See choke coil.

Inductance coil—A coil of wire so arranged as to have a large amount of inductance.

Induction—The transfer of electric or magnetic energy from an electrified body by proximity without contact.

Insulator—A material through which electricity will only pass when under great pressure, in many cases, apparently, not at all.

Kenotron—A trade name for a rectifying vacuum tube.

Key—The transmitting key is a switch by which the primary circuit of transformer may be readily and rapidly made and broken.

Kilowatt—One thousand watts.

Laminated—Composed of a number of thin plates placed one on top of each other with enamel insulation between.

Lead-in—That portion of the antenna circuit from aerial to instruments.

Lead-in Insulator—Any form of insulator used for passing down-leads of the aerial through the roof or walls of operating room.

Loaded aerial—One whose electrical length or frequency is artificially varied by adding capacity or inductance, or both, in series with the antenna circuit.

Loading coil—An inductance coil used to artificially "lengthen" an aerial.

Loop aerial—A large coil used in place of an antenna system to intercept radio signals.

Magnet—A piece of iron or steel, having the power to attract other small pieces.

Megohm—One million ohms.

Meter—Fundamental unit of length in the metric system. Equal to 39.37 inches. Used in radio for the measurement of wave length or space covered by one cycle of transmitted electrical energy.

Microfarad—Mfd. Practical unit of capacity. One-millionth of a farad.

Modulation—Variation of amplitude of radiated energy from a continuous wave sending station. May be done with buzzer, chopper, microphone, external oscillator, etc.

Motor generator—Consists of a motor directly coupled to and driving a dynamo.

Natural wave length—Length of wave produced by aerial's own induction and capacity. In single and parallel wire aerials horizontal or perpendicular, wave length is about four and a quarter times the length of meters of aerial. In a T aerial, about two and a half times. In the umbrella type, about five times.

Ohm—Unit of resistance. Resistance offered by a column of mercury at temperature of melting ice, 14,452 grammes in mass of constant cross section, and having a length of 106.3 cms. Circuit has resistance of one ohm when one volt is required to force a current of one ampere through it. Voltage divided by amperage gives ohms.

Ohm's law—Current is directly proportional to pressure and inversely proportional to resistance of circuit. Current in amperes is equal to pressure in volts, divided by resistance in ohms.

One-stage amplifier—Amplifier in which one vacuum tube only is used.

Oscillating current—Alternating current having a frequency of hundreds of thousands, or even millions, per second.

Open circuit—One whose extremities are not connected to each other. A battery is on open circuit when it is neither charging nor discharging, i. e. idle. Electrically incomplete.

Parallel—When two or more paths are open to a current, they are said to be in parallel.

Phantom aerial—An artificial aerial, consisting of concentrated capacity and inductance used to test a transmitter without radiating much energy.

Phase—An alternating current is in phase when maximum E. M. F. and current are reached at same moment. Two things are in phase when they occur at the same time.

Phone—Abbreviation for telephone.

Plate circuit—That circuit in a vacuum tube receiver in which the amplified current flows.

Potentiometer—A device for tapping off any desired fraction of a voltage applied to its terminals. Distinct from an ordinary variable resistance, inasmuch as it is shunted across circuit whose potential it is required to regulate.

Quenched gap—One which causes a quick breakdown of the conductive vapor bridge between discharges after passage of a spark by cooling of the electrodes. Any gap which does this may be loosely termed "quenched," though the term is more particularly applied to one consisting of a number of small gaps in series between comparatively large metal disc electrodes which radiate the heat.

Quenched spark—A form of spark, which owing to the arrangement of the discharger extinguishes itself rapidly after allowing a few oscillations to pass, thus permitting the secondary or aerial circuit to oscillate with its own natural frequency without interacting with the primary.

Antenna resistance—The total resistance of the antenna system, including the direct current resistance and A. C. impedance.

Radiation resistance—The factor determining the radiated energy.

Radio-frequencies—Frequencies higher than audio-frequencies, that is, over ten thousand cycles per second.

Radio-telephony—Transmission of speech or music by means of electromagnetic ether waves.

Reactance—The impedance, experienced by a current in a coil of wire other than the ohmic resistance due to that current reacting on itself by induction.

Resistance—The inherent opposition a conductor offers to the flow of an electric current. The unit is an ohm which allows but one ampere to flow when one volt is applied.

Rheostat—A variable resistance used in series connection in a circuit to vary current flowing.

Selectivity—Having the power of selecting any particular wave length from a number, to the exclusion of the others.

Series—A number of instruments or cells connected up in a circuit so that the current must pass through each conductor successively.

Sharp tuning—Exists where a very slight alteration of the tuner produces a marked effect in the strength of received signals.

Short circuit—One having a very small amount of resistance. To cut out resistance of instruments of a circuit.

Silicon—Si. Non-metallic element. Grayish metallic looking substance. Fused silicon is a potential crystal rectifier and as such is used in contact with copper, antimony, arsenic, bismuth, gold and steel.

Slider—The sliding contact used for varying amount used of an inductance resistance coil or potentiometer.

Spark gap—Generally applied to a gap, about 1-64 inch, inserted across the primary coil of the radio receiving set to pass static charges to earth without damaging the set. In other words a safety gap. In damped wave transmitters, spark gap is the generator of the damped waves because it allows the secondary condenser to build up a high potential, then break down the gap and discharge an oscillatory current until the condenser potential falls too low to break down the gap resistance. This oscillatory current produces one wave train in the aerial. Other wave trains follow as the condenser builds up again and the process is repeated.

Telephone receiver—An instrument having a disc of soft iron (diaphragm) held over and near to an electromagnet, whose windings are such that very weak electric currents will cause disc to be vibrated, attraction and retraction of this diaphragm producing audible sound waves. Those used in radio generally have a permanent steel magnet with projecting soft iron pole pieces, which serve as the cores of the electromagnets. Thus the diaphragm is always slightly attracted and even a weak current passing through the windings will cause a considerable vibration to be set up.

Telephone condenser—A small capacity condenser used to by-pass radio frequency currents around the telephone receiver.

Thermo-ammeter—One in which current to be measured is caused to heat the junction of a thermo-couple, the voltage so generated indicating strength of passing current. Should not be confused with hot-wire ammeters, which are much less reliable or efficient.

Transformer—An instrument similar in action and construction to an induction coil, inasmuch as there are two separate coils, one having few turns and the other many turns, placed together to permit of induction and having a common laminated core. No core is used when employed to transform radio frequencies.

Transmitter—A device for converting sound waves into electrical vibration. The opposite of receiver. Also used to denote a set of apparatus used to transmit radio signals.

Tuner—An instrument capable of various adjustments of induction and capacity in the receiving circuit, thus permitting the reception of widely varying wave lengths.

Tuning coil—An inductance coil used to "tune" a circuit in order that it may respond to oscillations of various frequencies.

Two-stage amplifier—Amplifier in which two tubes are used.

Undamped—A train of oscillations of constant amplitude. Having no damping.

Unit of capacity—See capacity.

Unit of Potential—See volt.

Unit of resistance—See ohm.

Unit construction—Individual pieces of apparatus assembled together to make a receiving or sending set, all parts being interconnected both physically and electrically by means of standard connectors.

Unloaded aerial—One having no added capacity or inductance for tuning purposes.

V. T.—An abbreviation for vacuum tube.

Vacuum—A space entirely devoid of all matter. The term is also lightly applied to spaces which are only partially devoid of matter.

Vacuum tube—A device composed of cathode (filament), anode (plate) and grid (auxiliary anode) enclosed in a highly evacuated glass bulb. Operates as a rectifier, amplifier or detector of small alternating currents when the cathode is heated and the correct potential applied between the cathode and anode. For detection, the bulb may have a small gas content which increases the sensitivity.

Vario coupler—Term broadly applied to any device for regulating the amount of energy transformed from one circuit to another by alternating the degree of coupling between these two circuits. Circuits may be either direct or inductively coupled. Substitute for receiving transformer or loose coupler.

Variometer—A continuously variable inductance made by revolving a coil within or near another.

Volt—That electric pressure which steadily applied to a resistance of one ohm allows a current of one ampere to pass.

Voltameter—A combination of voltmeter and ammeter.

Voltmeter—Instrument for measuring voltage of circuit. Connected across main leads.

Watt—Unit of electric power. To find power, multiply voltage by amperage. Kilowatt equals thousand watts; 746 watts are one electric horsepower.

Watt-hour—Commercial unit of electric work. Is work done in one hour by current of one ampere flowing between two points of a conductor having a difference of potential of one volt.

Wave changer—A switching device used to rapidly change the length of the wave being transmitted.

Wave length—Distance between two successive antinodes in same direction. An antenna tuned to receive is determined by the length of antenna circuit and loading inductance and capacity.

Wave-meter—A variable tuned circuit consisting of inductance and capacity in series with an indicating device to show resonance with an exciting circuit. Calibrated in meters or cycles (frequency) for determination of wave length in sending or receiving station.

Woods metal—A soft alloy, consisting of two parts lead, one part tin, four parts bismuth, and one part cadmium. It melts, at about 70 degrees Centigrade or 150 degrees Fahrenheit.

CB537B

Printed in the United States
101767LV00005B/319-321/A